Rewiring Not generations through elder wisdom, story and legacy

Stories by
Residents and Friends of
Villa Maria Manor
Independent Living
Senior Residence,
Nashville, TN
Selected and Written by
Ann S. Harris

TABLE OF CONTENTS

Dedication 1

Foreword 2

Preface 4

Story and Writing: When Ink and Imagination Make Magic 9
  By Ann Harris

PERSEVERANCE 11

Reinventing Myself 12
  Story by Bobbi Albert

Imagination and Story 15
  Story by Ann Harris

Laimute: Introduction 18
  Story By Laima Dickens

Juliette 19
  Story by Juliette McMahon

Attitude is Everything 22

The Dancer, The Rose, and A Toad: A Whimsical Tale .. 23
  Story by Brenda Nichols

GRATITUDE 26

Thank You So Much 27

The Gift of the Cedar Chest 28
  Story by Ann Harris

Carefree *33*
    Poem by Ann Harris

Closure: A Time for Healing *35*
    By Ann Harris

Holy Laughter *36*
    Story by Shoshana Abraham

Ready to Move On *38*
    (as shared by a church parishioner)

COURAGE *39*

Is It Time? *40*
    Poem by Ann Harris

The Courage To Hold Fast *42*
    Story by Bobbi Albert

The Walkway We Trod: A Whimsical Tale *45*
    Story by Ann Harris

A SENIOR INDEPENDENT-LIVING RESIDENCE: Where Community and Creativity Come Together. *49*

Sources of Renewal *50*

Watch Your Garden Grow *50*

Write Your Story *50*

Paint Your Canvas *51*

Arts/Crafts *51*

Knitters/Crocheters/Stitchers *52*

Discover New Worlds *52*

The Resident Council *52*

Keeping a Social Life *53*

Happy Hatters *53*

Keeping Fit *54*

Celebrations and Gatherings *54*

When First I Awoke *55*

   Poem By Wanda Bumpus

When Extra Help is Needed *56*

Bingo *56*

When Sorrow and Grief Overshadow One's Spirit *56*

FAMILY CONNECTIONS *58*

A Layover to Catch Meddlers *59*

   Story By Bobbi Albert

Mama's Prized Possession *61*

   Story by Lisa Atkinson

Picasso in Vallauris *65*

   Story by Annie Pardo

Heartbreak On The Prairie *69*

   Story by Brenda Nichols

The Observer *73*

Story by Ann Harris

If I Ever Send You Flowers 77

Story by Brenda Nichols

Rupert's Christmas Journey: A Whimsical Tale 81

Story by Sue Duplessis

Senior Perspectives For Younger Generations 84

Partner Up! In Intergenerational Dialogue 85

By Ann Harris

Seniors, Irreplaceable Treasures:Here To Be Valued

Story by Jean Marie Albert, an experienced nursing professional

Mother 90

Poem by Brenda G. Hall

"Blessings Within": Equality Prophesy 91

By Betty C. Dudney

An Intergalactic Visit 94

Story by Betty C. Dudney

Voices For Our Time: An Elder's Perspective 96

By Ann Harris

The Bay: A Sacred Place 104

Story by Ann Harris

Loss of Innocence 108

Story by Bobbi Albert

Estuary—a place of culmination, imagination, and creative gift: An Interpretation 111

By Ann Harris

Ode to the Estuary 114

Poem by Ann Harris

A New Day Arises from COVID 116

By Ann Harris

CONCLUSION 118

REFLECTION ON SENIOR STATEMENTS AND IMAGES with Commentary by the Late Fred Rogers 119

Contributing Authors 125

RESOURCES 128

When the River Meets the Sea 134

Connecting generations through elder wisdom, story and legacy

Dedication

This book is dedicated to Adult Children who face the challenge of caring for their elders. It is a daunting task to consider difficult and costly choices over an unknown length of time. It involves juggling jobs, providing for family and growing children, and all the related financial implications these considerations foster. I respect, applaud, encourage, and ask for God's blessing on all their efforts to compassionately care for those they love.

Magnolia blossom. Acrylic by Ann Harris.

Foreword

It is a privilege to journey with the seniors living at Villa Maria Manor. I have deep respect for those who have willingly provided writings in this collection that reflect on their experiences, the seasons of life they have weathered, the lessons they have learned, and the joys and sorrows they have walked through. I believe the reader will also find there is much to learn from the wisdom of these authors. I have come to understand that as people age, they become more vulnerable and thus a more authentic version of themselves. An authenticity that is refreshing and invigorating.

Much research has been done on cultures where populations experience the greatest longevity. One common denominator in these communities is the celebration of the elderly. In the U.S. culture, there is often a tendency to believe that as people age, they lose their purpose, their value is lessened, and they are less of a necessity and asset to the world.

The authors of stories in this collection are seeking to rediscover purpose and find resiliency from challenging life circumstances. Their contributions bring life to a broad scope of human emotions.

Brené Brown challenges us in her book *Braving the Wilderness* to "move in...hold hands with strangers." For many, seniors are strangers. The contributions provided in these pages draw the general population closer to seniors through their own words.

Connecting generations through elder wisdom, story and legacy

As I read and re-read these pages, I am inspired by the richness and insights of those who have journeyed along life's path further than I have. The stories and thoughts shared in this small volume are from seniors who are creatively navigating this challenging season of their lives.

Julie Bolles
Staff Counsellor
Villa Maria Manor

*First white iris of the season.
Acrylic by A. Harris.*

Preface

Senior living is hard. "It's not for sissies" is heard often from the lips of those over 70. In these unorthodox pages are images of lives being lived at the elderly end of the human spectrum; glimpses of abundance, grace, joy, grief, loss, illness, despair, challenges, loneliness, depression, spirit-filled, gratitude, and legacy. All of that. It is the realization that a life lived into senior years accumulates a wealth of skills and knowledge – a base of inner wisdom on which to draw.

I recently became an octogenarian and have been retired for some years. I am able to ambulate, though not without pain, piece together jigsaw and crossword puzzles, drive city streets, and enjoy an afternoon movie or meal with friends who are reasonably active and those who are not, physically and mentally. I am aware, however, that my current circumstances can significantly alter in an instant. I've witnessed these sudden turns into surgeries and conditions that cause dramatic change, increased mental and physical limitations, and the need for more skilled care. This is an integral part of the elderly life. How do elders navigate these changes? As best they can within the parameters of resources, emotional support, and services available, and out of the strength of their faith and a desire to be part of life.

I speak as a senior, having lived through decades of experiences, as have the seniors who are represented in this work through their writings. The stories are examples of the value and ability to give the community insights arising from the wealth of living into advanced years.

Three primary issues are raised that closely touch senior lives today:

Connecting generations through elder wisdom, story and legacy

1. The burgeoning senior population has increased the immediate need for housing with truly affordable services and amenities. One such senior independent living option is Villa Maria Manor, a HUD-subsidized facility administered by the Catholic Diocese of Nashville. The Villa is one inspiration behind this book. Its activities and offerings are described in some detail.

   The American independent living and skilled care communities for the senior population, especially for those with limited resources, vary in quality of care, breadth of services, and activities. Continuum of quality elder care should be on any politician's or community leader's priority list to keep the public focused on this vital segment of society.

   Residences under the Affordable Housing Act through HUD are the most reasonably priced at prorated monthly rates based on formula calculations for each resident. Descriptions of activities available at Villa Maria Manor where I have lived for three years give an idea of what to look for when searching for residential options for yourself or a loved one. Please refer to the Resources section for a brief advisement on actions necessary for transition to a senior residential lifestyle.

2. Public perceptions of senior life have needed an overhaul for some time. Breaking down the barriers between generational groups is a hopeful goal that can bridge the gap between the desire to access experience (the desire of younger generations) and to share current and technological trends (what seniors need from younger generations). These exchanges can lead to a healthier society--each meeting the need of the other. Supporting

the wellbeing of seniors makes possible collaborative opportunities to address the needs of all segments of the community in the future.

3. The power of story brings glimpses of local and global lifestyles into being, revealing truths that can influence the quality of community life and health for the better. *Rewiring Not Retiring: Connecting generations through elder wisdom, story and legacy* shares stories written by seniors living at Villa Maria and other affiliations, that arise from the richness of personal experiences and complement the commentary. They present family events in different locations, courageous stories overcoming life's challenges, and amusing anecdotes that make you smile—all telling tales that make up a poignant legacy. Throughout this book, writers' personal recollections are crafted into heartfelt tales that illustrate the commonality of their stories, the power of the written word, and the source of a living legacy.

When I entered semi-retirement in my early 70s, I discovered an enormously rich community that is generous and giving, contributing hours of time and resources to projects that benefit many. Now in full retirement, I am surrounded by resident craftsmanship and unique abilities. It is long past due to equalize the living field by bringing attention to the wisdom and knowledge of the senior population and to return seniors to the respected place they once held and deserve.

It would be well to periodically ask, "Where are the protectors of the dignity of advancing years?" Are we as individuals of any age, doing our part to respond to the needs of seniors we know? Are our churches helping to fill this role?

Connecting generations through elder wisdom, story and legacy

Do the citizens of our city and councils have the welfare of elders on their agendas? To keep up with actions in the political and municipal realms, "Bookmark" on personal computers groups that monitor, collect, and communicate information about deliberations and bills proposed by bodies such as a Metro Council and at state and national levels.

Walt Whitman (1819 to 1892) is one of America's most celebrated writers. He describes Old Age as "the estuary that enlarges and spreads itself grandly as it pours into the Great Sea." I find this image fascinating because this is exactly what I have been experiencing for the past few years. It is an exciting place to be but has a habit of introducing new ways of thinking about the world and its events that create challenges, and doubts about "the old" and tend to steer my energies toward fatigue. But if given the choice again to engage or not to engage, I would choose to be in the very same place! Later in the book I have written a commentary on Whitman's imaginative quote.

Three characteristics—perseverance, gratitude and courage—are most prevalent among the senior population. Applying these three words into the context of the senior world presents a vital community waiting to be engaged. The sections under these descriptive headings provide stories and commentaries on how each of these character strengths is strongly represented in the senior community.

Globally, several cultures honor their elders, hold them in high esteem and respect, and make room for them in their homes, attending to their physical and emotional needs. Domestic and resettled communities with these standards have set examples of such family structures for the elderly in our country. Responsibilities are shared among family members. The loneliness that generally accompanies "old age" is lessened in the presence of growing children and others in the household. Elders become part of the home and contribute their life-long experiences and time to help family life. But this may not be the best solution for all seniors, even if the opportunity exists.

Senior residences can be places where residents experience enjoyment, provide for the local community in many ways, and receive some recognition for their contributions. Supportive residential environments can exist with Resident Councils or Resident leadership in some form or through administrative staff offering a variety of programs for the creative, purposeful senior. A representative volunteer council can give substantial voice and life to the needs and interests of residents.

I am deeply grateful for the expertise of Patricia Hall in assisting with the formatting of the original manuscript. My thanks also for the commitment of time and attention to detail from readers of the manuscript and their helpful comments. A special thank you to Bobbi Albert who patiently listened to each piece as it was pulled off the printer!

So, our journey into elderly living begins. You may want to grab a rollator, walker, or sturdy walking stick to assist you in navigating our pathways.

Ann S. Harris,
Author and Editor

Connecting generations through elder wisdom, story and legacy

Story and Writing: When Ink and Imagination Make Magic

By Ann Harris

I picked up a pen and started writing in my mid-sixties after a long drive south of Nashville on Interstate 24 with no destination in mind. Mile after mile I mentally sketched my first cat-inspired adventure! And I haven't put the pen down since. I got as far as the exit sign to Bell Buckle and turned west. Intrigued with the town, I stayed for lunch and used the restaurant's paper napkins to start the first of several kitty stories that took place in my West Nashville backyard and neighborhood.

The core cast of characters were cat companions that lived with me over three decades in New York, Montana and Nashville, TN. Acting as a team, they solved any mystery and returned a turbulent neighborhood to peace and tranquility.

The central focus of the action was a critter-dug hole under the backyard chain link fence through which cats and small dogs could travel at will—on a path that led to pastures, woodland trails, neighbors' back doors and other destinations created only by imagination.

Now, I'm listening to stories by the writers of the Villa Maria Manor Writer's Group. Creative souls who have put their hearts and imaginations to work starting in 2022 during COVID-19 days. Stories of childhood or family country weddings, a summer on the Côte d'Azur. Or ones that combine three disparate elements into whimsical, comical, delightful tales! Where an elf, or a prima donna ballerina, a world-famous jockey, or a toad has a strange adventure and accomplishes its dream using a unique skill the character possesses.

It's a privilege to be part of this group surrounded by stories and relishing the wonder-filled transformation brought to the author, the reader, and the listener-- when ink, paper, and imagination make magic.

Blue iris. Acrylic by A. Harris.

Connecting generations through elder wisdom, story and legacy

PERSEVERANCE

Senior living is a time of constant perseverance. This reality, whether it materializes at 60, 70, or 80 years of age, is a definitive change in living style. Increased doctor's appointments, consumption of daily pharmaceuticals, changes in stamina and physical abilities, perhaps requiring aids such as rollators or walking devices, and loss of mental agility--are all indicators that one is now "elderly". Grace comes in acceptance of this reality. There are specific changes indicating phases of human maturing, and growing limitations of previous modes of operation become crystal clear! Perseverance becomes routine, ongoing, daily.

Vase filled with palette knife blooms.
Acrylic by A. Harris

Reinventing Myself

Story by Bobbi Albert

Who am I? Who am I, now that my children are grown? Who am I, now that I no longer have a career? Who am I, now that my grandchildren no longer need me? Who am I, now that I have sold my house and moved into a Senior Living Facility?

For most of my adult life, I knew who I was—I was my husband's wife, my children's mother. Then, I was a professional woman with an interesting and rewarding career. Even after I retired, I was involved with my grandchildren—keeping them on weekends, picking them up at school, watching them during the summer while their parents worked. Along with other activities in my life, I was busy, involved, and fulfilled. Then, one day—I know it wasn't just one day, but it seemed that way—I was no longer needed. Those grandchildren who had filled my life for the past years since my retirement were growing up—they were busy with their own lives. I did not know who I was.

As I was wallowing in my depression, one of my sons came by to talk with me. He said something that changed the direction of my life.

"Mom, you have to reinvent yourself. That's what I had to do when I got my life back together."

This particular son is an addict. At the age of forty, he hit bottom and, with the help of God, managed to get clean and has been that way for fourteen years. Although he had been a successful professional, at his lowest, he had lost his job, his family, his children—everything that was dear to him. After his rehabilitation, he managed to get a job and work his way up to a promising career again—it was not difficult to take advice from him. He really did know what he was talking about.

So, I did reinvent myself. It was really exhilarating to be doing something "just for me" without having to think about how I would impact any significant others! I threw myself into my church, my friends, my garden, my hobbies, and my extended family. For more than ten years, I was content with my life. But at the age of almost eighty I was facing a dilemma again; this time because I was selling my home of fifteen years and moving into a Senior Living Facility. Now, I realized I did not know who I was again! Once more I needed to reinvent myself.

But, can I do it? Even though I had been successful several decades before, it seemed daunting this time, a task I don't feel up to. I had back surgery prior to moving here and suffer from complications that have impacted my lifestyle. Over two years into my residency here, I am assailed by self-doubts and a crisis of self-confidence. I know that now is the time: I can't keep putting it off. Time has a way of flying by, and if I don't act before I know it, I will end up unhappy and discontented for the remainder of my years. But this time, it is scary. I don't know where to start. I have friends here. My family is supportive and devoted to me. Yet, I struggle. Who am I? At the age of eighty, will I be able to reinvent myself again?

I know that the answer to the question "Who am I?" lies within myself…what I make up my mind to do. I believe that thoughts dictate actions. As a wise counselor told me recently, I have a choice. I can choose to wallow in my unhappiness, or I can find ways to reinvent myself…again! I can enjoy my friends. I can get involved in activities that are available to me here at the Villa. I can join in streaming events that are available to me. And most importantly, I can decide to be content.

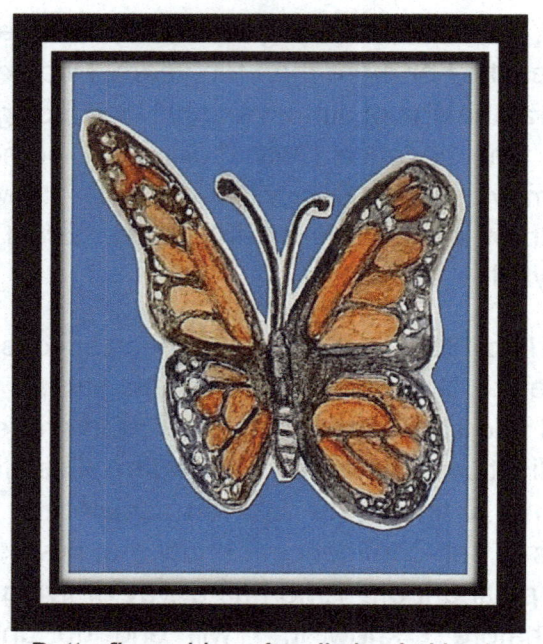

Butterfly on blue. Acrylic by A. Harris.

Imagination and Story

Story by Ann Harris

I met Rita in the elementary school Resource Room. She was sitting in front of an antiquated computer monitor with a pile of children's storybooks on her left and open pages of *Clifford the Big Red Dog* on her right. She was composing simple questions about the story of a huge dog who manages to save the day from disasters. These were questions for her young readers to ponder and answer.

Rita typed, "Where was Clifford's hiding place?" and "How did Clifford solve the mystery?"

Rita wrote questions for each book in the school's *Reading is Fun* program, a weekly lending library for kindergarteners through fifth graders. The students checked out a book for a week and brought it back with the completed questionnaire to earn points for prizes later in the school year. As the book was returned, the student could select a new one for the next week.

Rita was a wiz at these question sheets. This project was "her baby." In her so-called retirement years, she loved her part-time volunteer job of bringing each story to life from the most elemental picture book to a pre-teen chapter book. The kids loved the challenge and loved Rita.

"Rita, how long have you been writing up these questions?" I asked one afternoon when she finished the sheet for a newly donated book.

"Six years. Love every minute of it. I can tell you about any book on the shelves. I do have my favorites, though. When I can, I change the questions to keep interest in the book fresh. The kids tell me their parents and siblings help the younger readers with their books and question sheets at home. Isn't that great?"

Coming in and out of the Resource Room regularly during the school year, I couldn't help but notice that Rita's face and squinting eyes were very close to the screen and that she had significantly increased the font size of her screen work. I asked her about this one day.

"Yes, you're right. I seem to be having difficulty seeing the screen clearly. I think the school needs to replace this monitor. It's been here almost as long as I have. It has to be wearing out – just like me in one way or another!"

Then, Rita received news about her diminishing eyesight--she was in stages of macular degeneration. The bare fact was there was no cure or hope for improvement of this condition.

"What am I going to do? This is not going to get any better. I know that. The monitor isn't the problem, of course. I'm not aware of a technology that can help me deal with this. I can still create the questions but it's harder and harder for me to read the books. Magnifiers are so cumbersome and not strong enough. The only books I can read are the large print early readers and picture books."

With each passing week, Rita seemed to lose her joy in the *Reading is Fun* program and eventually made the tough, rough decision to let this precious project go to someone else.

When that happened, the Resource Room lost its most dedicated champion of the reading program and the person who helped the children excitedly check out books each week.

Through common church-related interests, we shared some community activities. Rita retreated from a life-filled schedule of her former days.

Then something changed, slowly at first and then in a more pronounced way. Smiles became more frequent. She said that she decided to adopt "life" instead of "despair."

Rita is reading books – all kinds of books—with the aid of an illuminated jeweler's loupe, a tool that gives her the gift of the printed word. Reading is part of her life once again. Rita is a woman of hope and determination who writes beautifully in large cursive letters. Her humorous, sensitive writings have become her legacy to family and the community. She is bringing life to those around her just as she stirred the imaginations of the school children instilling in them a love of books, stories, and wonderful world of reading.

Laimute: Introduction

Story By Laima Dickens

Introduction. I am breathing easier now at age 72. I can sense calm and serenity in my life for the first time. I realize after decades of tumultuous living; I am thankful for all the "second chances" I've been given to help me develop a sense of control--and a solid base for living in this beautiful world.

I've come from a chaotic past that began at the end of World War II in Europe. I have survived a traumatic and destructive childhood that produced lasting psychological and physical damage. Over many decades, I suffered physical, mental, emotional, and drug abuse, but in the midst of those horrors, always striving toward a better life for myself.

It's time now to remember and make peace with all I have endured over seven decades of living. It begins with a little girl in Germany named Laimute Marya Jakutis. It frightens me to bring up and relive these disturbing and unsettling years, but it is necessary—therapeutic--to face the fears of my past and finally put them to rest. Honestly, I am amazed I have survived it all. But in so doing, I hope to offer you, fellow traveler, a glimpse into how my struggle may relate to yours in some ways, and how steadfast love and courage can bring sufferers of pain out of darkness to the light.

Connecting generations through elder wisdom, story and legacy

Juliette

Story by Juliette McMahon

[Editor's Note: Juliette was invited to give a report at a Knights of Columbus evening program event. In preparation for her talk, she prepared a set of laminated note cards from which she spoke.]

Good evening. I was asked to talk to you about my struggles and successes in life. Grade school was a constant struggle for me. I always used to stand and watch the other kids play. When they said I was too short I took what they said as the truth. While watching the kids play, I would sing to myself a song called Playmate which I had heard before. When things got overwhelming to me, I would start daydreaming, and for a little while I would forget my problems. When I went to school there were too many in the class. I would stay after school and ride the bus home to get extra help. I also went for speech. I sang in the choir by listening not by reading the music. I was always told as a kid by my father, that if I could only be half as good as my brother, I would be OK. According to some neighbors my brother and I were least likely to succeed. We both are college graduates.

I was always placed in the next grade. I asked someone in my class what that means, and they said, "If you do good, they keep you, and if not, you go back." So, I never had a sense of belonging.

In High School, there was only one person who offered to help me by giving me an oral test instead of a written one. But people were complaining, and he had to stop. In my second year, I was on the winning basketball team. The other teams had to throw us a banquet. That was one of the highlights of that year.

I worked at Steak and Shake as a car hop. I found out from a co-worker that I didn't need a High School diploma to go to beauty school. I wanted to succeed at something, so I went to beauty school over the summer. I never went back to regular school. I was 16. I learned to give permanents and cut hair. When it was time to test for the state board, I passed. I did perms and haircuts for the elderly and disabled in their homes.

Everything else seemed to be going OK. I was married and had two children, a daughter and a son. I did a lot of volunteering but also stayed in the background. My confidence started to drop. My children brought their friends home. I wondered how they had so many, recalling how few I had at that age.

A friend took me to a church program. I learned a lot by listening. The speaker was from KCC, the Alive Program. It took me a few days to get up enough courage to call and make an appointment for literacy counseling. I was ashamed and embarrassed that I didn't read like everyone else. It took a lot of dedication, determination, and a real commitment to work toward my goal. I wanted to call it quits on many occasions. My tutor, however, helped me through those times. She stayed with me until I received my GED. It was the proudest day of my life when I walked the aisle to receive my GED.

I used to be afraid to talk to a group of three, but the first time I spoke to a group was at my own graduation. Later, when serving as chairman of the Teachers Recognition

Banquet, I completed the DOORS program, which helped me gain confidence in myself. But I failed the KCC test. I fell apart. I realized that what I was focusing on was what I couldn't do and not what I wanted to do.

I started the Alive program in 1987, achieved my GED and a Certificate in Early Childhood, and graduated in 1997 with an associate degree. I achieved my 10-year goal! I still struggle today. Some think because I am a college graduate, I can do anything. But I know I learn better by being shown than learning out of a manual.

My Motto is: I want to give back to society what society gave to me: a new beginning. By speaking out on behalf of the Alive Program at a variety of places, I have met this goal. Kids thinking about dropping out of school decide not to after hearing me talk. I would not be where I am today without the help I received from the Alive Program and the support from family and friends. I continue to focus on what I can do and not on what I cannot do. Thank you.

Attitude is Everything

Meet a neighbor at the Villa who has just reached her seventh decade. Due to a severe car accident, she walks with a limp, and because of a head injury sustained in that accident, she has some cognitive impairment and is unable to work. Her quick, warm smile greets you on the elevator early in the morning as she takes one of her canine charges for a morning walk.

In her apartment, there are craft projects in progress and completed ones displayed on the walls. She is not deeply into her elder years but shares their limitations. As an example of a positive attitude, she takes on a "can-do," "participatory," and "social" approach to life. My neighbor earns a few extra dollars by walking two resident dogs daily. This responsibility brings her out of her apartment, keeps her body moving outdoors, and allows her to socialize while exercising. She usually seeks a craft project to start.

I have not heard or seen this resident overly complain. She accepts her limitations, knows what she can do, and makes the most of her day. She is an inspiration to others. Most of us have probably been at the unpleasant receiving end of negativity. It is refreshing and uplifting to experience someone who is aware of the positive effects of a good attitude.

Character: A prima donna dancer
Skill: Teach a toad how to boogie
Dream: Win an award for a prize rose.

The Dancer, The Rose, and A Toad: A Whimsical Tale

Story by Brenda Nichols

Rosemary was trying out for a dance part in a play at her community theater. She had taken dance classes year after year because her mother wanted her to be a prima donna dancer. She liked to dance and tried out for many dance productions. She was never quite good enough to get the part.

She had been practicing her moves for this audition all week. She thought she was ready. As she went on stage to find her place she stumbled and hit the floor like a stack of wobbly toy blocks. You see, Rosemary's balance was never quite on point.

Next, she was to do the positions required for this dance. The director told her to try the Arabesque position, a one-leg stand, with the body in a straight line. She did the Attitude position instead, with one leg bent at a 90-degree angle. She could tell by the director's face that she didn't get the part.

Discouraged she left thinking, *I must find something I can do better.* Rosemary decided to go home and sit in her garden on her green metal bench and reflect on what she could do.

She could smell the heavenly scent of roses before she even got to her garden. She loved the roses that God gave her the talent to grow. The yellow was her favorite. It was her mother's favorite, too. As she stared at the beautiful flowers her mind drifted to her dream that she had as a child while helping her mother tend the plants that would produce so much joy for them both.

She wanted to win the prestigious Garden Club's Prize Rose Award. She could see the judge studying her yellow rose, the color of the midday sun. The moisture content of the petals enhanced the hues and brightness of the yellow. There was a perfect spiral from center to edge, with each petal in its place. The stem was long and straight, with foliage evenly distributed.

Then something caught her eye, bringing her mind back to where she was. She heard a raspy voice and saw a plump little toad.

"Oh My! Who are you? she asked.

To her surprise, the little guy with little webbed feet over his eyes answered in tears,

"I am Timmy, and I can't boogie."

In a kind voice, Rosemary said, "Why do you want to boogie?

Timmy explained. "There is a lily pad dance and catered dinner on the other side of the pond tomorrow. All toads in the pond must Boogie dance from pad to pad across the pond to get to Grandaddy's pad for dinner. And there's a trophy for the one who Boogies the best."

Rosemary exclaimed, "I can dance and do the Boogie. I

will teach you. It will be more fun than those fancy dances."

She got up and put a rose in her mouth, freeing her hands to help her balance. Her hips went side to side and around and around as she shook all over. Her feet were moving so fast they looked like a blur to Timmy. Timmy jumped up and down clapping and ribbiting and began to follow her moves. He went faster and faster with his little webbed feet flying back and forth. His plump tummy swiveled around and around, ending with a jump to a stepping stone.

Rosemary yelled, "You did it!"

Timmy insisted Rosemary go to the Grandaddy Lily Pad for dinner and dancing. Rosemary agreed. And as she sat on the slippery Lily Pad, here came Timmy around the bend doing the Boogie dance from pad to pad, all smiles and doing little twirls on each. When he came to the Grandaddy pad, he did a flying summersault onto it. The crowd cheered and the trophy was awarded to Timmy. He hopped over to Rosemary giving her a yellow rose and an envelope from the Garden Club with a certificate for First Place for the yellow rose from her garden, as well as membership to the Garden Club. She was overwhelmed and tears fell.

Then the dinner bell rang. There was a distant sound of humming. Rosemary thought the dinner music had begun. Then she noticed that all the toads were quiet with their tongues out waiting. She looked up and saw it. A big cloud of mosquitoes!

She screamed, "I am allergic to mosquitos!" She grabbed her gifts, slipping and sliding to the shore, and ran all the way home in fright. Rosemary and Timmy saw each other often in her garden, but they never went to dinner together again!

GRATITUDE

These stories illustrate aspects of the sense of gratitude that pervades personal exchanges and acknowledge the small kindnesses and considerations found in the community of residents at the Villa. This frame of mind, this action stems from the acceptance of the conditions of elder years and becomes a positive attitudinal benchmark of the senior community.

The story, poem, and shared pieces that follow express genuine gratitude for small offerings of thoughtful acts, gratitude for a new understanding of one long departed, a stress-free drive through the countryside, and the gift of touch that brings special comfort.

Seahorses: Acrylic by A. Harris.

Thank You So Much

"Thank you so much for the soup. I'm feeling better today."

"I appreciate you taking the time to check on me. That means a lot to me."

"I'm going to the store. May I get you something?"

"I thought you might like to read this book; it's a real cliffhanger."

"I've got an extra chocolate pie in the freezer. May I bring it to you when your sister comes over tonight?"

These comments are more the rule than the exception at the residence. They make me breathe easier as I go about my day, knowing that there are kindnesses in abundance within the building. This is a community and the gratitude flows both ways from person to person, from person to dog, from cat to owner, friend to friend, from a relative stranger to new resident, to someone who has lived at the Villa for many years.

Now, don't get me wrong; there are countable situations where the generous spirit stays hidden. But compassion is catching, replicating itself even in spite of an ill-spirited thought or deed.

The Gift of the Cedar Chest

Story by Ann Harris

The Cedar Chest was no ordinary piece of storage furniture. Its contents had been stored away for over 50 years, out of sight, forgotten. Opening it revealed another world—clothing from a distant era, fragrances from an earlier time, and the discovery of a truth many decades later.

"What is this?" I asked myself as I entered the basement -- a sweaty sixth grader, home from school on a hot Friday in June.

In front of me was a polished wooden storage chest. It took my breath away with its shiny locks and latches and brass fittings covering its rounded corners.

I put my bookbag on the concrete floor next to the mystery chest and tried to open the lid. A sudden waft of lavender filled my nostrils. Before me, neatly folded, was a collection of clothes and accessories from an earlier century. *Oh my, these things are beautiful.* I moved a few items from one side of the chest to the other. A second waft of sweet cedar mixed with lavender surrounded me.

I carefully lifted out a lacey cream-colored ivory fan, opened it dramatically, and cooled my face with its gentle, soothing breeze.

"Anns, did I hear you come in?" asked Mother, using the name my family calls me, from the upstairs kitchen through the open door to the basement.

"Yes, Mom, I'm here. What is this chest doing here? It must have arrived today."

"It came from Honesdale. Grandma Suydam's things. You remember that she passed away a month ago. Come upstairs and help me with supper, please." Mom's strong voice requested.

Dinner table conversation centered around the delivery of the chest that day.

"Grandma's things have been in storage for many years, ever since she moved into the nursing home ten years ago. Her belongings haven't seen the light of day for some fifty years. These are her wedding clothes, shoes, fans, gloves—that sort of thing," Mother explained.

"Family thought that Dad would like to have them—since they belonged to his mother. We'll need to decide on what to do with them."

"MAY I HAVE THEM!? I'LL BE VERY CAREFUL WITH THEM! PL-E-A-S-E," I immediately asked.

Dad replied, "Hold on, Anns. We'll need to check out some possibilities on how to best dispose of them."

That night I thought about the last time I saw Grandma Suydam. It was not a pleasant recollection. She had slipped me a large black pill saying to take it to keep me regular. Whatever that meant. She used a metal tool on my fingernails to "make them look neater" but it hurt. I don't think she meant to hurt me, but that was Grandma.

Dad would talk about his mother in her earlier family days,

"It's a shame you didn't know her when she was much younger. She was slim and beautiful in her own way. She thought that she was unattractive because of her darker skin tone."

Mother added, "She always seemed to be trying to keep her curly hair under control with hairpins."

Then Dad: "In most family photos, Louise would be partly hidden behind whoever was in front of her. She believed her attributes did not fit the fashion of her day."

I spent the weekend in the basement admiring the floor-length, now off-white silk wedding dress. The bodice was laden with tiny pearls in swirls across the front to the slender waistline. In the back, covered silk buttons fitted into their loops from the neck down to below the waistline. The silk clothing must have been made on the looms of the silk factory near Honesdale that Grandpa ran until it closed and was sold in 1929.

When we heard of Grandma's passing, I remember Dad saying that work was hard to find at that time, and Grandpa finally took a reporter job with a Brooklyn newspaper, far from home, and a loving wife in Honesdale. Louise learned that her husband had died suddenly while on assignment. It was 1936. He was 55; she was 49. Grandma never recovered emotionally from this event. She moved into a guest house in town and stayed there until she needed nursing care.

In the night's stillness, I recalled these recent conversations and slipped down to the basement--raised the lid of the chest. Lavender and cedar. *I wondered, What did Grandma wear after the factory closed?* I picked up the satin buttoned shoes and the long fine net veil with pearl studded hairpins. I thought of young Grandma Louise, and her unruly curly hair--JUST LIKE MINE. On the face of a chromed framed mirror, looking back at me was an olive-complected face-- JUST LIKE LOUISE.

My middle name is "Louise." I knew I had been named after Grandma, and now I fully realized why.

I related to my grandmother at this moment more than any other time. We were kin and shared similarities of naturally curly hair, olive-toned skin, and probably more. The difference was that my attributes were acceptable in the fashion of my day.

By sharing and handling her clothes from a time when she was an energetic mother and a well-respected hostess of Honesdale society, I felt I knew her better and could forgive her quirky habits later in life. I pictured her trying to survive a financial loss, the loss of her husband, and leaving her home alone. Wiping the tears of better understanding away from my face, I closed the lid of the chest. I sat quietly beside its holdings of her beautiful things. Amid the lavender and cedar fragrances, I said softly in the dim light,

"I love you, Grandma!"

Rewiring Not Retiring

Cedar chest from Honesdale. Acrylic by A. Harris

Connecting generations through elder wisdom, story and legacy

Carefree

Poem by Ann Harris

She calls and asks
"Do you have
sometime today
to drive somewhere,
maybe that shop
not far away?
So I can step outside
my apartment for a bit."
"Sure." I replied, "Let's stretch
our legs to try to keep fit!"
"Perhaps visit places we've
never been before.
To a metro park, a museum,
a new store."
I want to make some
free time just for my friend.
We've enjoyed these treks now
for many months on end.
Our times together clear out
our clogged mental spaces,
bring wonder and carefree smiles
to our faces.
The hours before us become
an artist's canvas
welcoming new brush strokes
with each mile that passes.

The route is set with whimsy
as our guide

taking detours that veer off from
side to side.
It's a time that invites
a good deal of laughter.
"It's the best thing to do,"
we always say after.
We might stop and shop,
or have coffee and chat
and talk about lots of things—
about this and that.

Our searching for words and
sense doesn't matter.
We enjoy dearly our banter,
our chatter.
We're glad to be together,
sharing what we do.
Just my friend and I.
And God's there, too.

Photo by A. Harris.

Connecting generations through elder wisdom, story and legacy

Closure: A Time for Healing

By Ann Harris

Sometimes "closure" is a painful word. A word, however, that can bring a place of peace and rest, particularly in elder years when closure helps to complete one's life journey in dealing with "unfinished business."

The words of an unresolved issue may come unexpectedly--no warning, no preparation. Tears may flow from the intense emotion they cause. Feelings may erupt from words that dredge up old conflicts, hurts, disappointments, and a realization that their effects are still lingering in the background of life. Their emergence may overtake you again for a while as you pour out your feelings.

Hold fast to their arrival and this "pouring out". Stay with the pain of release. Keep writing or praying the words that fill your entire being, until the outpouring begins to subside and you sense a peace—the peace of release— that speaks from the soul. And you realize that you have let go of past hurt by entering those feelings and perhaps by acknowledging deep sorrow and regret. These confessions, this encounter with the past, lead you to a place of honesty, forgiveness, openness, mercy, and love. You have been drawn into this encounter to deal with a lost or fractured relationship or a farewell that has not been said and has been due for a long time.

Gratitude enters this place of healing, along with acceptance and a wider understanding of circumstances. Gratitude stills the soul. This grace of freedom lightens the heart and brings brighter clarity.

Holy Laughter

Story by Shoshana Abraham

A small-statured man standing on stage reminded them of the stand-up comedian, George Burns, minus the cigar. His unique speaking style provoked the audience to break out into laughter and tears, all within a deeply profound lecture.

This speaker was a well-known ob/gyn physician who over the years had delivered hundreds of tiny new souls into this world. He was filled with miraculous stories from which he had learned great lessons. His profession had never ceased to amaze him. It had instilled in him an awareness and clear understandings of life's sanctity and balance.

He took nothing for granted and his words imparted and filled his audience with the same gratitude and essence. An awakening began to dawn which evolved into a naturally unifying caring and respect. What was happening within this group--this newfound "family"--was LOVE! The doctor's talk was on "Love." Right there in the lecture hall was a union of souls who hungered for love.

As the physician continued to speak, a woman in the audience broke out into loud and hearty laughter. This reaction became contagious and one person after another caught the laughter. In many different styles the room erupted in snorts, giggles, pounding the floor, belly-holding shakes, that no one could stop. Some begged it to cease but it went on until it petered out—leaving all in the room exhausted, spent and happy.

Through all of this the speaker remained silent, observing and smiling. He knew from where this exuberance had been sent. A healing gift of love. When one woman didn't get off the floor and settle back in her seat, he continued to wrap up the lecture. When the evening's program ended many were exchanging names and phone numbers, hugging and promising continued contact and the bond of friendship. The last three women remaining in the hall noticed the woman still lying peacefully on the floor. Not wanting to disturb her, they turned the lights off and tip-toed out of the room.

The woman later told her story. Laying on the floor during that night, a divine presence came and sat down beside her taking her right hand, saying, "I love you, Rachael, young gazelle." His inaudible voice saturated her with His indescribable love, which rang true and loud, not in decibels but in strength. She cried for a long while, humbled and filled with love and gratitude. He had delivered to her His mercy and caring such as she could never have imagined existed; an experience within her heart that had changed her life; an occurrence she would never, ever forget.

How wonderous was this unexpected encounter during a Women's Retreat which provided amazing respite for a young mother of three children.

Ready to Move On

(as shared by a church parishioner)

My friend talked about visiting her 106-year-old grandmother who lived in a nursing home in the Midwest.

"She is dressed nicely for our visit in blue slacks and a floral blouse. The colors brightened up her room which was filled with photos of favorite memories.

"Her faith has been her bulwark. She lives a life of grace. She is always a delight to be with. But now, sitting in her wheelchair, very present to me, it is clear she would rather be with her Lord."

"My hands ache. My body aches," she quietly shares.

I move closer to her and start to gently massage her upper legs. "Tell me if this is uncomfortable for you, Granny. Let me know if I am pressing too hard."

"Oh no. This feels wonderful, dear." She had long since not recalled my name.

Human touch. How soothing it can be. A beautiful act we can do for each other. It is a simple gift we can offer. Especially for those who seldom receive it.

Drooping Tulips. Acrylic by A. Harris.

Connecting generations through elder wisdom, story and legacy

COURAGE

Courage, a strong characteristic of the elderly, keeps seniors moving through daily living. It's the strength that allows the continuance of a purposeful existence. The interior fire of courage is the driving force of the older population.

Considerations about retirement and the arrival of the concept of the older adult, senior citizen, and elder, raise the question "Is It Time?" Perhaps one of the first indicators of entering into this phase of life is "the downsize."

The Swift, Agile Swallow. Acrylic by A. Harris

Is It Time?

Poem by Ann Harris

Is it time to make the BIG DOWNSIZE?
Is the time right? Is it really wise?
Inwardly I hear words of Ecclesiastes
from various verses in Chapter Three:
"For everything under heaven, there is a season." (3:1)
Is it time for a deep review to examine the reason
for recurring thoughts of end-of-life and health,
workplace successes and diminishing wealth?
"A time to build up; a time to break apart." (3:3b)
Listen to God. Listen to my heart.
Sit still, reflect, hear what's next.
Absorb, digest, accept the context.

Simplify home; reduce the clutter.
Sell the rake and grass cutter.
Rummage through closets, dispose of excesses.
Give away wrong-sized shirts and dresses.
Sell what you can, donate the rest.
Believe it or not, it's for the best.

Am I ready for transformation? God's new deal?
The emotions are hard and difficult to feel.
Releasing past regimens that have worked for me,
on a well-traveled path of self-sufficiency.
Now, in new territory—this independent living—
I meet people with walkers and wheelchairs giving
their greetings: "Hello" and "How are you?"
They make me feel welcome from my new view
in a high-rise community, safe and secure.

Connecting generations through elder wisdom, story and legacy

This kind of inevitability is sure.

New opportunities, relationships and more
are waiting for discovery on every floor.
Friendly residents, one by one,
share a greeting on an elevator run
to where my reduced things fit nicely and snug.
Gone are the buffet and dining room rug.
There's no room for each family-held piece.
They're memories now as my holdings decrease.

Instill in me warmth and mirth
that transformation brings to birth.
A new era has begun, a new day rises
filled with new friends and endless surprises.

"God has made everything beautiful in time" [3:11]
 as I now enter this new paradigm.

The Courage To Hold Fast

Story by Bobbi Albert

*It takes courage to stand tall to hold fast
to one's ground in a world forever spinning.
We say "This is my place. I'm safe here. I will stay."
But sometimes, a tempest comes and
whips the Earth up from our roots.
We stand diminished and exposed. We are known.
We are naked. And we tremble at the prospect
of the next shift of the elements.*

From "Call the Midwife Season 10, Episode 7. Aired January 2021, BBC."

The video camera was recording. The nurses and therapists clapped and called out with glee—some even cried--as they watched the woman hesitantly take her first step unaided. The woman was terrified. She was afraid she would fall. She had spent two months in a hospital and three months in a rehabilitation center. She had been paralyzed from her torso down—only her arms and neck had been spared from the relentless effects of the unexpected event that had, like a tempest, changed her life forever…overnight. Truth be told, the staff had not expected her to walk again; however, she had spent these past months holding fast to the hope that she would. Jamie had recently had back surgery, a not-uncommon procedure for a woman her age. She was recuperating when she suddenly was unable to move. Testing showed that the metal that had been placed in her back had broken, and much like dominos that fall one after another, two ribs, one on either side of her spine, had splintered off. Jamie was paralyzed. Emergency surgery was performed. When she woke up, she was still paralyzed.

Relentlessly, the days passed with little progress. Her legs would no longer straighten because of muscle atrophy. She lay in a hospital bed, wondering if she really would be able to walk again. Depression set in, a profound depression borne of pain and uncertainty.

Jamie had been raised in a religious household and had a deep faith. So, she prayed…and prayed…and prayed. At first, her prayers were frantic, asking God to heal her, to let her walk again, to restore her to her previous health. But then, as time passed, her prayers began to change. One day as she talked with God, she finally was able to put it in His Hands to ask Him to heal her if it was His will, but if not, to help her accept that her life would never be the same, that she would not recover. After she was able to turn it over to God, she felt a sense of peace descend for the first time since her surgery.

With renewed courage and drive, Jamie threw herself into her physical therapy. Now Jamie walks gingerly, because should she fall, irreparable damage would be done. She still has residual impairments: she can't bend over because her back is metal from her sacrum to her neck. Her balance isn't as good as it was previously, but she is thankful that God answered her prayers.

As she walks today, bakes today, spends time with her grandchildren, family, and friends, those all around her admire and silently applaud her courage to hold fast.

Perched owl. Acrylic by A. Harris.

Character: Armless acrobat
Skill: Can paint with my toes
Dream: As poet laureate, perform at the next presidential inauguration

The Walkway We Trod: A Whimsical Tale

Story by Ann Harris

I didn't think it would ever be possible, but in the technology age, I guess solutions can come out of nowhere if there is interest in exploring the possibilities.

Phocomelia is the condition you have if you are born without arms. This is how I, Jonathan Perkins, entered this world on a warm July morning. The dysfunctional remnants of misshaped hands were surgically removed, leaving a full shoulder. My parents were horrified, they told me later, but there was never a day that they didn't applaud an accomplishment or encourage me to try something new. Their support and love were boundless.

Born without arms, my upper body had to rely on my torso, head, neck, and shoulder muscles to maneuver me through the day. My legs were the strongest part of my body and because of the dexterity of my toes and the muscles of my foot and ankle, they compensated in many ways for the lack of upper limbs.

I didn't have many friends in school, but there were a few kids who overlooked my obvious handicap and befriended me. They got accustomed to my strange ways of doing things and even joined me in laughing at some of the predicaments I got myself into.

I guess I thrive on trying to do the impossible, but there were times in elementary school when I almost felt "normal." In a 4th grade gym class, the teacher, for some reason, included me in a class exercise of rope climbing. I looked at that long thick rope hanging from a huge hook installed in the ceiling and started to wrap the rope around my neck. I found that I could flip my body upside-down, holding and tightening the rope around my head, ears, and neck in a loop, and use my legs and toes to shimmy up the rope almost as fast as my classmates could right-side-up!! I learned quickly that I had to keep my weight really slim so I wasn't carrying any extra fat or my neck couldn't hold the loop with my whole weight pressing down on it.

I became a "boy wonder" in gym class, and won all kinds of prizes in running races around the track at school events. Later in junior high, I was so busy on the athletic team representing my school at competitions that I didn't have time for any self-pity! It didn't hurt either that my looks weren't all that bad except for some obvious missing upper-body appendages!

My family kept after me to try painting. Yes, painting! With the fine-tuned dexterity of my toes, I really could draw some credible shapes. So, adding colors, this froggy is one fun attempt.

There were companies that offered to design instruments or apparatus to allow me to accomplish an ordinary activity, like driving a car! I drove my second-hand lime green Mazda with a modified steering wheel in the form of a joystick! My knees shifted their position to turn corners, change gears, back up, parallel park, and all the rest. My friends and family didn't even feel terrified when I was "behind the wheel".

As I got older, into my early twenties, my life became more public. My unusual abilities became known. Various groups in town wanted to hear "my story" and I was invited to talk before all kinds of gatherings. I started to feel the necessity to write about my gratitude for the amazing support and interest I had already received from my family, teachers, friends, and the community! I joined a writer's group at the community center and began to put my thoughts on paper—with my toes, of course!

I just celebrated my fortieth birthday at a small party my wife organized with our neighbor friends. I can't tell you how thankful I am for my beautiful partner, Katie. We are a great team and have been for 12 years. We have two kids who are, I hastily add, physically normal. It takes both of us to try "the impossible" of keeping our household moving along fairly smoothly! I am thankful every day for my life and for those who have been by my side and on the periphery.

This year I am honored beyond belief. I've been asked as a member of the National Handicapped Association of America to read a poem I have written at the upcoming Presidential Inauguration! Can you beat that? Jonathan Perkins, NHAA poet laureate, in front of millions. I end with a brief excerpt:

*When we think of this country and its endless
wonders,
its citizens, cultures, and colors we live under,
we see a land where impossibilities are transformed
into possibilities for
all—not a few. Reborn
in solidarity to found strong communities, cities
and a nation that is sound.*

*We strive to work
together, holding up
what we love and preserving what is good.
We continue to foster and
build healthy neighborhoods.
May Mercy and Justice and the great love of our God,
hold us in harmony, unity
and bless the walkway
we trod.*

Connecting generations through elder wisdom, story and legacy

A SENIOR INDEPENDENT-LIVING RESIDENCE: Where Community and Creativity Come Together.

The eight-floor mid-rise building in midtown Nashville houses 214 senior citizens aged 62 and above, providing a safe, well-maintained home environment. It does not offer a common dining room. Meal preparation is within resident apartments.

Villa Maria Manor is an attractive HUD-subsidized residential community that simplifies home living in one-bedroom apartments affording residents freedom from the responsibilities of home property maintenance. There is a limited number of handicap-accessible apartments as well as a few two-bedroom options for couples.

*Potted Eggplant in Villa Garden,
With Residence in the Background.
Acrylic by A. Harris.*

Sources of Renewal

The community that forms around activities at the Villa is a unique one. Villa Maria Manor is the only senior residence in the Nashville area that has a Resident Council composed of resident volunteer leaders. It is a source of limited financial and social support for an array of activities centered around the interests of the residents. The following descriptions are samplings of the gifts and opportunities currently within the Villa Maria community and are offered as an example of a senior independent living residence option.

Watch Your Garden Grow

The summer garden is a sight that delights: lettuce, squash, tomatoes, okra, herbs, and more. Many residents participate in tending their plants and often sit around the shaded tables at the garden's edge to socialize while caring for them. A table invitation reads:

Photo by A. Harris.

*Come celebrate our garden that is
growing nearby.
Enjoy these shaded tables and let
blossoms catch your eye.
Sit down for a while and peruse the peaceful view.
Restful garden moments are
waiting here for you!*

Write Your Story

Put pen to paper and write, write, write—passing on your stories about yourself, your loved ones, places, and people you have known. Create a story legacy for the generations that follow. Make discoveries about yourself and those you write about, enriching your understanding. In time for the 2022 holiday season, a printed booklet of selected stories written during 2022 classes was launched. What a wonderful way to celebrate the writing skills of the group and provide a gift option for residents, friends and family.

Paint Your Canvas

A *Plein Air* painting group has an early spring project of creating and painting floral designs on the exterior of three olive barrels that provide the water supply for the garden vegetables and flowerpots. All paints and brushes were provided. Bring your ideas and join the fun. Or sign up for the monthly Classic Creations Class featuring a guided painting experience.

Arts/Crafts

A seasonal craft project of creating a canvas and felt wall hanging Advent calendar was scheduled for four sessions during November 2021. Six residents completed a green felt tree and a pocket holding 25 miniature ornaments with a natural canvas backing ready to hang for a countdown to Christmas! This project is sure to put crafters in the holiday spirit! Or perhaps make a pinecone wreath for a gift or decoration on your apartment door.

Knitters/Crocheters/Stitchers

Gather for a congenial time together to learn how to knit, crochet, and macrame, and enjoy each other's company. Come to a semi-annual craft sale at the Villa, and you will see the amazing skills of the residents. Items created meet needs across the whole life spectrum from birth to elder years with everything priced very reasonably. No need to shop at commercial outlets for stitchery gifts. The Villa sales tables will take care of your holiday and special events gift needs!

Miniature knitted koala bears.

Discover New Worlds

Book Review, music, and monthly art Classic Creations groups are available to discover new areas of interest. Why not try a new activity to expand your skills and increase personal enjoyment?

The Resident Council

The Resident Council meets monthly to review/discuss the activities of the residence, volunteer opportunities, educational/ organizational presentations, operational concerns and guidelines, programmatic offerings, and budgetary reporting.

Five officers (President, Vice-President, Treasurer, Secretary, and Hospitality/Sunshine coordinators) oversee the Council activities in coordination with the Villa Manager and Administrator.

The breadth and success of activities on the calendar speak to the effectiveness of the Council's purpose, the commitment of its Officers, and the willingness of residents to volunteer to lead and participate in the offerings.

Keeping a Social Life

Catching up with the daily newspaper in the Activities Room over a cup of coffee entertains some residents for hours each morning; others join in the conversation just for company. Occasional movies in the Activities Room, Sunday Church services, and musical groups perform for residents a couple of times a week.

Happy Hatters

It was Happy Hatters Luncheon Day. The ladies gathered in the lobby of the Villa to sort out transportation coordination to the restaurant. Not being a member of this social group, I lingered in the lobby watching car ride assignments materialize. The last car departed, heading toward Charlotte Avenue on its way to its destination, Cracker Barrel at 12:30 p.m.

What stayed in my mind was how everyone looked fabulous, with a hat adding the finishing touch to an outfit. I marvel at how much time and effort must have been spent by those women to accomplish such stunning results! The lobby, now empty of people, has around its perimeter a lineup of walkers and rollators awaiting the Happy Hatters' return in a couple of hours.

Keeping Fit

In mid-morning, the Activities Director enters the Activities Room to lead a small group in a 35-minute chair exercise class, offered twice a week. The set of exercises, designed by a nearby physical therapy clinic, keeps resident bodies moving! And MOVEMENT is the name of the game! The twice-weekly routine can be attended in person or viewed by way of an in-house TV channel in a resident's apartment. An updated exercise room will be operational in 2024.

Celebrations and Gatherings

Activities led by the staff counselor feature surprise or announced topics each week: current events, places to visit, or sharing experiences and laughter. You leave these meetings knowing your neighbors a little better, mentally stimulated, and more energized for the day.

Attend a community-wide meal celebrating a holiday or birthday or events providing grief support, where a small cash or food contribution makes these gatherings possible. Other events are scheduled for Vendor-sponsored meetings with topics such as phone service, health insurance and medical plans, financial organization, and fraud prevention.

Birthday/special occasion celebrations. A resident celebrated her eightieth birthday in a gathering of 60 relatives and friends in the Villa Maria Activities Room. She wrote this poem in the early morning on her birthday.

Connecting generations through elder wisdom, story and legacy

When First I Awoke

Poem By Wanda Bumpus

When first I awoke this morning
on this my 80th year
I was a bit melancholy—
my 80th birthday was here.
And then I thought if I'm very still,
And if I closed my eyes,
And if I don't look in the mirror,
I could be 25!
I could be that girl again,
so young and alive!
In this cool and quiet room
I could be 25.
Then I began to feel better.
Suddenly I didn't mind
not being as young as I used to be
and not being 25!
All day I held on to that
feeling,
And finally realized
it will be as good to be 80
as it was to be 25! (well almost)

When Extra Help is Needed

After some observation and interaction, it may become clear that a resident or family member is no longer thinking clearly or appropriately. This is a sadness that occurs in senior living as it does in homes out in the community. Someone is slipping mentally and emotionally and may not be able to reliably care for oneself. It is then that the social worker or physician actively enters the scenario and suggests to the family that help be made available to assist the elder to remain compliant with meds and ensure the individual's safety. Eventually, this may mean a move to a nursing or skilled care facility. These changes are difficult to witness and personally experience.

Bingo

Bingo is offered once or twice a month, either in person in the Activities Room or remotely in apartments on Senior TV. Bingo is a favorite activity that draws a crowd; better yet if you win a roll of paper towels or bath tissue while participating!

When Sorrow and Grief Overshadow One's Spirit

In the senior mid-rise, the death of a resident is a certain reality. There are several deaths that occur in a year's time. This is, of course, sometimes forecasted with Hospice Care attending to a family member, but sometimes it is sudden and a shock. News of a death is communicated quickly, and all can know the general circumstances with the family's permission. The staff are well aware of procedures and remain calm and responsive as the situation requires. Services are scheduled, prayers and words of comfort are shared, and a photo is displayed in the lobby, memorializing

Connecting generations through elder wisdom, story and legacy

the deceased loved one for a period of time. All of these actions leave residents with the opportunity to grieve those who have passed and left friends, pets, and family behind.

The Shepherdess.
Watercolor by A. Harris.

FAMILY CONNECTIONS

The following several stories connect family in special moments with parents, grandparents, children, extended family, and neighbors: the love of a grandfather for his young granddaughter; outings with an elderly mother and her favorite purse; a summer vacation in the south of France; a sudden death within a farming community; a family celebration during Christmas holidays; and sustaining love of a spouse who remains steadfast with her husband through his mental illness. The last story in this section is a whimsical one made up of three disparate elements that the writer makes into a coherent, delightful tale.

The environment of home, although often flawed, is the center of human existence. Story is a conveyer of these formative settings where humanity starts life and goes on to mature in the elder years. Family is a life-long relationship that connects us from one generation to the next.

Swan family. Acrylic, A. Harris.

Connecting generations through elder wisdom, story and legacy

A Layover to Catch Meddlers

Story By Bobbi Albert

"What are you making? Is it for me?" The little girl could scarcely contain her excitement as she pranced around the room. Her grandfather was making something out of wood—something small and shaped like a chest. She was sure it was for her. All he would tell her was that it was "a layover to catch meddlers." How could she know what that meant? She was only seven years old.

The grandfather labored in his small, cramped workspace. He had cut the wood for the project outside but as it was December, he was putting the pieces together inside the house. His granddaughter was excited and curious. She kept pestering him, trying to wear him down to get him to reveal what he was making. In fact, it was for her—a doll chifforobe. He knew she loved her dolls! Her mother and grandmother made clothes for them. This would give her a place to store them. But to keep her guessing, he kept giving her an answer that she couldn't possibly understand, "a layover to catch meddlers."

On Christmas morning, the little girl ran to the living room to see what "Santa" had brought her. There, under the tree, was the present her grandfather had made her— a "layover to catch meddlers." A doll chifforobe! She recognized it as a place to store clothes. Her great-grandmother, who lived with them, had a chifforobe in her room because she did not have a closet. Now, she had a place to store her doll's clothes. She played with her dolls all the time—they were her babies. She got them up in the morning, dressed them, and put them to bed in their pajamas at night.

The little girl used the doll chifforobe lovingly during her childhood years. But, as she grew up and her interests changed, childhood treasures became unimportant and neglected. Her grandfather passed away, and as the years marched on, the doll chifforobe was moved many times and weathered adverse conditions.

But age tends to bring much of life into focus and those things that were dear to us earlier in life tend to gain significance again. During my last move, I unearthed the chifforobe once again and set out to restore it to its former glory--all it took was some Murphy's Oil Soap and Minwax. Yes, the mirror is dimmed and there are a few nicks on the frame, but otherwise it is still standing tall and proud.

So, what is a "layover to catch meddlers?" Was it just something my grandfather made up to keep me from pestering him? On a whim, I looked it up on the Internet. Surprisingly, it was there! The "Morris Dictionary of Word and Phrase Origins" by William and Mary Morris states: "layover to catch meddlers" is a dialect variant of a common answer used by adults to evade a direct answer to children's questions instead of saying to the child "it's none of your business" or "shoo." Well, this cryptic response certainly achieved that purpose! And now many years later as I remember the love and skill that my grandfather put into making the doll chifforobe and his enigmatic way of deflecting my curiosity, the "layover to catch meddlers" is on display and makes me smile.

Connecting generations through elder wisdom, story and legacy

Mama's Prized Possession

Story by Lisa Atkinson

In her elder years, my mother lived at Still Hopes Retirement Home in Columbia, South Carolina. I visited several times a year for a few weeks from my home in El Paso, TX. Hopes was an attractive place, progressive in its programming for seniors, offering a variety of activities and a pleasant dining room. But on my visits, we ate out a lot to get away from the usual dining room menu and enter back into the outside world away from the four walls of her apartment and, later on her assisted living room.

I met Mama at her apartment late in the morning and helped her gather a few things. Her purse was put securely into the basket under the rollator seat, a cardigan sweater for overly airconditioned places, and some tissues in case her nose needed attention. Her rollator fit snugly in the back seat of my car.

"Lisa, where are we going for lunch? How about that fine place with the wonderful gift store?"

"That sounds perfect, Mama. It's not too far from here. We'll be there before too long."

As we pulled out of the parking lot of the residence, Mama

asked with a fixed look in her eyes and a panicky quiver in her voice, "Lisa, Lisa, where's my purse?" This would be one of many times in the day when Mama's purse would be the focus of conversation and concern. With my assurances that it was safely in the back seat with her rollator, and Mama's quick look in that direction, we continued toward the restaurant.

Driving down the road, I recalled how I reached an understanding about her preoccupation with her purse in knowing that as a child she grew up in a desperately poor home and neighborhood. Coming from a previous generation of poverty, and the "doing without" extreme frugality of her parents, she blamed herself and her very existence as the cause of her family's poverty. She and her two younger brothers were always very sensitive to how poor they were.

Eventually, Mama became an English teacher throughout rural Iowa. Years later, she was appointed as Director of Advertising at Webster Publishing Co. in St. Louis. It was there that she met my father. After 8 years of meeting once a year (!), they married and settled in South Carolina. Mama never worked again. Their married life was always under the shadow of my father's own frugality, having lived through the Depression himself. My father never provided her with enough money to pay the house bills fully. Using some money left to her by her father ($40/quarter) coupled with $20/week from my father, who traveled his sales territory each week, she became creative with how to save and use the money available wisely.

"OK, Mama, we're here. I'll get your rollator out of the car. Then we can go inside and be seated at a table."

I extracted her rollator, collected her other belongings, and we entered the restaurant. Luckily, we were seated immediately. As Mama sat down, she put her purse over her head and let it hang across her chest within sight and touch.

"I think I'll put on my sweater. It's a bit chilly in here." I passed her sweater to her.

The hostess came and took our orders and left to place them into the queue. We sat comfortably across from each other, enjoying being together. I loved Mama so much. I could feel her love return. As we waited, we started to talk about how she lived a tightly controlled life under Daddy's financial constraints.

My father was home only on weekends, and many of my memories of family life were through the sweetness of Mama. I never felt that I lacked much. My siblings and I had a loving and caring home life; we had what was needed. She loved people and was so caring to those who needed help. Mama's life had been rich with friends from all parts of her life—even kindergarten.

When my father died, Mama surprisingly received an inheritance as the result of my father's frugal living and wise investments. It allowed her to live the rest of her days in relative comfort at Still Hopes Home. Her inheritance gave her a sense of freedom for the first time in her life, although she continued to be frugal herself.

Lunch arrived. "OOOh! I haven't eaten a fine hamburger like this in a long, long time! It's not on the menu at the residence."

After lunch, we spent some time looking through the gift

store. Mama found a piece of jewelry perfect for a neighbor at Still Hopes. We were soon back in the car on the return trip to Mama's residence; her purse was securely strapped across her chest.

Our conversation continued on the road. Not knowing about having extra things, Mama talked about her simple lifestyle in her one-room apartment and carried on the familiar patterns she had lived with all her life. Her extravagances and extras went easily to others more comfortably than to herself. She was generous to her family and to those in need or financial hardship, usually discreetly.

"Lisa, what a wonderful lunch with you today. Thank you, dear."

"I loved it, too, Mama. Be thinking about where you want to have lunch tomorrow."

As my sweet mother aged, her former fears of poverty returned as obsessive attention to her purse and its contents. Becoming increasingly fearful of losing what items she treasured as necessities, she developed an excessive attachment to any purse she carried. Her lipstick, breath mints, and tissue were all essential daily items. Her billfold, driver's license, one or two credit cards, a little cash, and checkbook were all necessary for orderly, responsible living.

These essential items easily occupied her 12" x 15" shoulder-strapped handbag.

I guess at the end of it all, none of us owns anything. Dust to dust... You can't take it with you... Or did Mama believe that the remainder of her independent identity was tucked away safely in her purse?

Connecting generations through elder wisdom, story and legacy

Picasso in Vallauris

Story by Annie Pardo

Poor teenagers!

You probably remember these years as a difficult time, too. Everything feels wrong, little nothings make you miserable or even ashamed. You feel you are on stage all the time and that the world is watching you. And so it was for me. Especially in the summers when I was with Raymonde, my grandmother. And now, when I think of it, I laugh, and those memories are dear.

1956. That year, Raymonde and I were on vacation in Vallauris, a famous village in the south of France, because Pablo Picasso had his pottery studio there for a time. It was a small village on the Côte d'Azur, between Cannes and Antibes, just 1.5 kilometers up the hill from the Mediterranean coast.

Was it the brightness of the sun? The happy sound of the bells of the Italianate-style church? Or the aroma of pissaladières[1] housewives were carrying home from the bakers' ovens? This scene was the Midi, so dear to us tourists. Our quirky efficiency apartment overlooked an outdoor café shaded by four linden trees and in the center Picasso's iconic sculpture, L'Homme au Mouton (Man with his Lamb). The 14-year-old me was left unimpressed by the peasant carrying a lamb in the crook of his arm, as I did not

---

[1] A specialty of Provence, France. Small thick rounds of bread filled with caramelized onions and anchovies and other ingredients

know yet what it meant. The sculpture was rough, and seemed unfinished, as if was made with handfuls of clay plastered on a figure and unpolished.

At this café, a local bus would pick up passengers to go down to the palm tree-lined beaches. If we were running late, Raymonde would make me hurry and tell the bus driver to wait for her, and she would come running. How embarrassed was I then; such an incongruous and undignified sight –my grandma, a short, rotund lady trying to run! Here, people have to demonstrate their reputation for joie de vivre and disdain for the rules. As she boarded the bus, the light-hearted driver would tell a joke about "Memere" for the pleasure of his passengers. That was the Midi.

It was summer on the Côte d'Azur and every day was festive. Posters mounted on the building walls announced the opening of a new Picasso exhibition. So, if you knew Raymonde, you knew we had to be there. This fiftyish, unsophisticated, petite Parisienne, who was never dazzled by celebrities, still enjoyed rubbing elbows with the glamourous, if only for the fun of it.

People were gathered on both sides of the street, and many more were by the gate to the exhibit. After a while, we saw Picasso coming down the street at the center of a crowd of Beautiful People. Naturally, the Master was surrounded by his "entourage"--friends and family, photographers, journalists, and extravagant characters of his court. For example, two young fellows walking side-by-side, each wearing a suit, a vertically bi-color black and white suit (one wearing the black side on his right side; and his companion on his left side.) Their heads were also half-shaved, each on opposite sides. All in the name of Art, I suppose. Their full

Connecting generations through elder wisdom, story and legacy

extent of eccentricities is not yet seen. The tableau before me was as arresting as a Master's painting.

In the crowd of gawkers, were Raymonde and me, admiring and dismissive of the celebrity. As Picasso approached us, Raymonde started foraging through her purse until she found a pen. "But what to write on?" She had nothing. She pulled from her wallet a photo of my mother feeding my baby brother his bottle.

As the Master, in his usual trademark white linen pants and sailor tee, was getting closer to us, some four or five steps away, Raymonde clasped my hand around the photo and pen and vigorously pushed me forward.

"Go! Go! Ask him for his autograph!"

"What? Me?" I said, mortified.

"I cannot do that! You do it!" I fought back; I had a high respect for the Arts!

As I was walking backward, she was pushing me forward until I fell into the old man's arms with my photo and pen in hand. This clumsy, awkward 14-year-old girl fell on top of the short man and pressed against his suntanned face and his gleaming crown of white hair. Oh! My! Everybody was watching and laughing. He, too, laughed good-humoredly, and turning around to face his public, he said holding up the photo,

"Look! How appropriate. A mother with child!"

With a flourish, he signed it and flippantly said a boutade [2] to his public.

I was thinking, *where are those photographers, now that I need them!* It would have been so marvelous to have a picture with the Master, even if I were in a ridiculous pose. The crowd pushed Pablo into the building along with his tightly packed company—with us in the middle. Ah, Raymonde. How could she embarrass me so? All the Picassos in the world would never impress the old working-class grandma.

Today, my daughter has this picture that Picasso signed. It has suffered a bath in spilled Coca-Cola, but the signature is still visible. It is Picasso's autograph, yes, but it's absolutely worthless. The Master had not drawn a single dash with his august hand. To me, its value is immense as it revives that souvenir of impervious Raymonde, my embarrassing but wise and proud grandmother in Vallauris.

---

[2] Boutade, a sudden loud outburst.

Connecting generations through elder wisdom, story and legacy

Heartbreak On The Prairie

Story by Brenda Nichols

Ella heard Bob, the faithful homestead's collie, barking franticly outside, running back and forth in the yard, making pitiful sorrowful noises.

Ella yelled, "Hush Bob, I do not have time for this! I need to work in the garden. I am coming."

He would not stop whimpering. When he saw Ella, he took off, skidding around the grain bin kicking up dust like a summer dirt devil. She followed Bob heading to the pole barn where her husband William was building storage for farm equipment and tools.

Suddenly, Ella saw the damaged roof of the shed that had caved in. She took off running as hard as her strong legs would take her. There he lay under a broken beam. Bob dropped down beside him whining sorrowfully. Ella dropped to her knees and checked his pulse, then collapsed beside him.

Finally coming to her senses, she realized she had to get help. She ran to the coral where she saw Molly her fastest horse. Ella whistled and opened the gate as Molly stopped in front of her. There was no time for a saddle. Ella jumped on bareback, grabbing the mane and kicking her legs as Molly flew across the pasture, taking Ella to find help.

The neighbor, Hank Fillio, was carrying a bucket from his barn as Molly came to a stop. Ella jumped off and said to him,

"Come, Help! William is not moving; he is out in the pole barn. Hurry!"

In one leap she was back on Molly racing toward home to be beside William. Hank soon arrived on his mule Rufus. Jumping off, he rushed into the barn breathless and saw Ella standing by William. When Hank determined William was gone, he took Ella by the shoulders.

"It is too late Ella." Her knees buckled, and she collapsed into his arms. Comforting her he said,

"Ella, we need to get Doc and the neighbors to help."

Looking up at him Ella replied,

"Hank, you go, Bob is here. I'll be all right while I wait with William."

Stunned, she walked shakily to a huge flat rock by the barn and sat down, Bob by her side. She remembered breakfast that morning, the last time she saw him alive.

Sobbing, she thought about her children. Each had their own special seat at the family table. Leta by her mama Ella, Irvin next, then Margarette beside Papa. That morning, they talked joyfully about how they would spend their day on the farm. Oh, what a wonderful Papa he had been.

Hank and Dr. Samuelson were soon back to help Ella to the house where her parents and neighbors were gathering on the porch to comfort one another. The doctor attended William and took him to town to prepare him for his funeral. A neighbor and Ella's parents brought the children home from school. They ran to Mama asking, "Where is Papa?"

Grandpa looked at his daughter, Ella. She nodded to her father to go ahead as she held the children to her. He took over and explained in a loving way what had happened. Ella said gratefully, "Thank you, Daddy."

She was thankful for her family's love and comfort, particularly on this day and the days to follow. William's parents lived in Missouri, so they received notice of death by telegram. His father came alone to Nebraska with William's brothers, John and Pete. His mother was unable to travel due to illness. Mourners came from miles around to pay their respects. William, a good man, was sorely missed by all.

Ella mourned deeply for William. Everything reminded her of him. As she did her chores, she asked God, "Why did this happen to our beautiful family that had a promising future?"

William was so strong in his faith when he shared it with their children. Ella clung to that faith, knowing he was in heaven. She was so thankful he was such a good example to their children, who now had that same faith.

The family, now four, had to haul water up and down hills from the creek to water the garden and for their household needs. Thankfully, the livestock could drink at the creek. If only there had been more time. The family was planning to dig a well. Ella reminisced about how fun and exciting it was to plan improvements for the farm. Now there was a big hole in each of their hearts.

The practice of neighbor helping neighbor had taken Ella and her family through these challenging times. Each neighbor began working at one farm, harvesting crops. Then they moved on to the next farm, putting hay in the barns and grain in the bins. This continued until each farm in the community had their work finished.

Farm work was hard, so an abundance of good healthy food was necessary. The women and young girls at each farm fed the workers. A hardy meal provided the strength for the workers to finish the day and a time to talk about their day's work.

Leta, Margarette and Irvin thought of their Papa often, remembering all the love he had given them, his fun personality and his talents. They cherished the days with Papa, Mama and all having supper around the kitchen table, each in their place. After the dishes were clean, they would retire to the parlor to talk about the day. Outside, Bob would curl up in his space by the front door and listen to the sounds of his family within. Papa would get out his fiddle and play songs. They danced and sang until all were exhausted. Bob headed off to his warm place in the barn. And the family climbed upstairs to sleep soundly to rest for tomorrow.

Connecting generations through elder wisdom, story and legacy

The Observer

Story by Ann Harris

"Come join us around the Christmas tree, Granny," invited her son, Paul.

Granny Louise stood up from her chair and joined the family circle. All ages gathered around the blinking lights of the festive tree prominently occupying her son's living room. Hanging ornaments, collected by Paul and his wife Amelia throughout their childhoods, filled the decorated tree branches with happy memories. Paul added a brilliant red glass globe inscribed with "Jason" so that it could be seen by nearly everyone. Three-month-old Jason was in the arms of his mother, Julie, Granny Louise's granddaughter. Proud Granny stood next to Julie and gazed into the bright blue eyes of her first great-grandson. Jason's sweet smile warmed her heart.

Paul and Amelia hosted the whole clan, still numbering 18, after a gain and loss of one family member during the past year. It was a blessing that all the family had settled within the area. No one had the expense of flights and accommodations from out-of-state or long drives from distant places.

So why was Granny Louise's mind so agitated? This was familiar territory. At age 88, she had enjoyed decades of family gatherings, raised three children with her husband, George, and for 45 years had a satisfying office career. Retirement came at age 70. She looked forward to spending subsequent years free of the scheduled hours under the office clock and the technology of the computer system she conquered when she abandoned her IBM Selectric typewriter as she entered the computer age so long ago! Looking back on her working days, there was something predictable, satisfying, and regular about family life and schedules. There was some comfort in knowing neighbors and friends were also juggling and managing the daily demands of children and workplaces.

A good while after retirement began, Granny noticed a growing unease arising out of the sameness of days-- sometimes welcome, sometimes dulling, mostly pleasant, at times challenging, and rarely- but certainly frightening. This last feeling had been increasing recently, mainly in the presence of family. The more family members around, the greater the sense of detachment, separateness, and even a little sadness. Why was that? Surrounding this day's boisterous activity of children and adult conversation was a soundless barrier: a silent, palpable space that separated the present moment into isolation. Louise was alone now since George passed away several months ago. She was also aware that she understood only bits and pieces of the sounds around her, even with her hearing aids. Everything else was blurred into unintelligible fragments.

During family gatherings at Paul's, the children and grandchildren came to her in her chair to give her a kiss on the cheek. She returned their restoring gestures with a bear hug, a smile, and an "I love you!" and away they'd go to do something else in their own worlds.

The family had long since gratefully bypassed her in any discussion of computer-related topics, particularly tech talk about iPhones, tablets, social media, and TV streaming – all of which she regarded as an amazing mystery! For some time, her thoughts concluded, "I'll stick to my favorite daily and weekly TV shows and my trusty landline phone. These machines are familiar to me and don't require those irritating passwords!"

The growing detachment was disturbing and, at times, even fearful. Was this going to be the pattern of her remaining days? She sat in her favorite winged-back chair at Paul's house, a chair everyone always left for her, knowing its firm structure supported her bowed back. It was comfortable to lean her head to the side and take a short nap.

Every day for the past six months, she thought about her partner in life. After 55 loved-filled years, George had slipped away peacefully in his sleep beside her. She knew the very instant his rhythmic breathing ceased. To ease her grief, she busied herself with her favorite pastime, knitting. She knitted, with precision, socks, gloves, matching scarves, and hats, preparing them for Christmas gifts. She had just finished a full layette for Jason, a gift she had completed for every Stewart infant over the years. There would be no exception for the newest member!

This morning, she decided, *"Today, I will not be concerned about those uneasy, distant feelings. It's Christmas Day, and I'm going to enjoy being with my beautiful family!*

Her greatest happiness was being among her loved ones, even when she felt like an observer on the sidelines. Maybe no one noticed. Even now, she felt the closeness of her beloved George right beside her; she just wouldn't be able to hold his hands or caress his smiling face. She deeply missed his touch. Yet, the warm memory of him at this moment dispelled any melancholy. In spite of his absence, all was well on this Christmas Day that held the joy of new life and a new generation!

Rewiring Not Retiring

Welcome to the next generation.

Connecting generations through elder wisdom, story and legacy

If I Ever Send You Flowers

Story by Brenda Nichols

We arrived to find out no one was home. Nick disappeared around the back of the house, where his uncle's motel was located. My two children and I sat by a tree, waiting for Nick to come back. We heard someone yelling. I looked up and saw Nick on the roof of the motel, screaming in anger,

"Why aren't they home? Everybody hates me, I will jump off this roof, and then you will be sorry."

More confusing, babbling, threatening words, came from his mouth as he raced from one edge of the roof to the other.

I pleaded, "Nick please come down, we can get you help! Please do not hurt yourself."

Then I became angry at the whole situation. I was madder than an old hen protecting her chicks from a fox in the barnyard and said,

"If you do not come down so we can get you help, I will leave and get the police."

Bee our eleven-year-old daughter, threw herself hysterically into me, screaming,

No, Momma, don't leave Daddy!"

"No, dear, we will not leave Daddy! He will get help."

Seven-year-old Johnny stepped up to the motel with his hands on his hips and, in a determined voice, asked, "Daddy!

Are you going to come down off that roof and keep our family together or what?"

Nick stopped in midstride, turned, and said:

"Johnny, call the police," then continued to babble incoherently.

The police were already in the parking lot and began convincing Nick to come down from the roof and took him to jail for the night.

Johnny asked, "Will daddy be ok now, Mommy?"

I took both children in my arms, telling them how proud I was of their courage and that Daddy was going to be all right.

That night, after supper, I tucked the kids in bed, then crawled into the bed next to them in the motel room. I was half in and out of sleep when I sat up with a jerk saying,

"He sent me flowers the day before we left home! Why?" He never gave me flowers! He hated flowers. He once told me that flowers reminded him of funerals and "If I ever give you flowers it's because I need help." I thought, *What? Was he serious? He had never given me flowers in all the years he knew me! It must be a cry for help.*

I tossed and turned most of the night, thinking about the 750-mile trip to Nick's family reunion. Nick's mental condition had deteriorated with each mile already traveled. His moods were as unstable as thistledown in a windstorm. The moods cycled from anger to crying to laughing to manic and driving erratically the whole trip. How could I get courage like my children had shown to deal with this crisis? How was I to help their Daddy?

The next morning, the Police explained that Nick was having a mental episode and they needed to get him to a mental hospital, which was 6 hours away and near the town where my parents lived. We followed the police car on the long trip to the hospital, watching Nick in the back seat making faces at us the whole way.

Grandma and Grandpa met us there and took Bee and Johnny to their home. I met the night nurse in the hall and heard Nick yelling. I saw him on the gurney in a straitjacket. He saw me and bellowed,

"I hate you, you put me in here. This is jail. You want to get rid of me! I want a divorce. Now!"

A mixture of sadness and determination made me walk over to him, my eyes filled with tears. Looking him in the eye, I said,

"No! Nick, I love you, I will not give you a divorce. I will be here every day to see you, whether you like it or not. When you get well, we will talk about it!"

They took him through the big green doors as I stood staring and shaking. It broke my heart to see the man I loved act like this. I heard him calling as they took him farther away from me.

"Boo!" the nickname he gave me so long ago, "Help me. I gave you flowers! Remember? I gave you flowers."

I stumbled to the front desk sobbing and told the nurse,

"I will be back in the morning."

As I turned to go, a spark of hope ignited within my chest. I thought, *could this be courage?* I hoped so. This may be a long, hard road ahead. And I whispered as confidently as I dared, "But I will help you."

Silver bouquet. Acrylic, A. Harris.

Connecting generations through elder wisdom, story and legacy

Character: Santa's Elf
Skill: Can hold breath for five minutes underwater
Dream: Space Travel

Rupert's Christmas Journey:
A Whimsical Tale

Story by Sue Duplessis

It was another hectic day in a quaint wooden workshop at the North Pole.

The workers inside were buzzing with activity to make ready the toys needed for the fast-approaching deadline of Christmas Day.

At the far end of one bench was a diminutive elf named Rupert. A toy rocket sat upright in front of him. Although a dedicated worker, he was lost in thought at the prospect of steering the craft into its space trajectory around the Earth, lost in a daydream of how it would be to soar into space in a real rocket.

This did not go unnoticed by Santa, who kept a watchful eye on the wellbeing of his employees.

"You seem distracted, Rupert. It may be a good idea for you to get away for a bit to rejuvenate your interest. I am going to promote you to a Reporter Elf. You will visit a family to observe the children to see who is naughty or nice."

Rupert nearly toppled over in excitement and in anticipation of such an adventure. Before you could say "Jack Frost" he was on his way to a place called Bayou

Manchac. It was very different from the North Pole. There was murky water everywhere with huge moss-covered trees and wildlife abounding. His destination was a small houseboat which was the home of the St. Amant family. Inside were Poppa and Mamere with their children Jean Claude and Gabriella.

Excitement was brewing as they were also preparing for the holidays. Much to be done! Pappa and Jean Claude were heading out to the pirogue to catch crabs for the gumbo. Mamere and Gabriella were making pralines for dessert.

The day flew by, and soon it was time to head to the levee for the Festival of the Bonfires. Upon arrival, they were greeted by their neighbors, who had also brought much food to add to the feast.

Just before midnight, the bonfires were lit to show Pappa Noel the way to the swamp families. Rupert took a seat on a thick iron ledge to see the festivities. As he leaned back to watch the fireworks, s*wish!* he slipped and fell inside a huge pot filled with water. When attempting to climb out, he was bombarded with onions, celery, corn, and seafood and was pinned underwater for about five minutes. Then, finally, he surfaced at the top. Dieu Merci! He was happy not to be the main ingredient for the gumbo! After going to midnight mass at the chapel in the swamp, the weary children returned home and hung their stockings along the houseboat rails, then fell asleep.

Soon Rupert heard the soft hooves of reindeer on the roof of the houseboat and knew his adventure was nearing an end. When he reached Santa's sleigh, he reported how helpful the children had been preparing for Christmas. Santa selected a beautiful doll for Gabriella and a fishing rod and reel for Jean Claude.

    Rupert was delighted when Santa told him that since he did such a good job, he would continue being a Reporter Elf. Rupert burst into a wide grin and thought, *who knows, maybe my next family will live on the moon!*

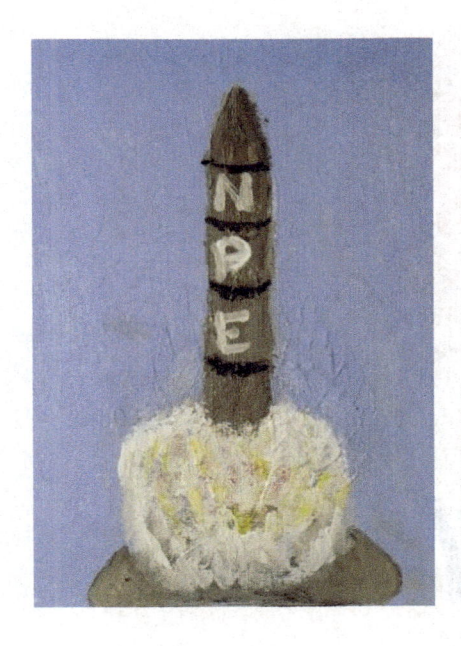

Today's news headline:
North Pole Enterprises spacecraft takes off from Santa's launchpad heading for the moon.

SENIOR PERSPECTIVES
FOR
YOUNGER GENERATIONS

Leaf in full seasonal colors. Acrylic, A. Harris.

Connecting generations through elder wisdom, story and legacy

Partner Up! In Intergenerational Dialogue

By Ann Harris

Story and commentary share perspectives that can set a pathway to unity and good will. This is possible to the degree that societies, nations, and communities collectively work toward common goals.

Within the group(s) you have chosen to affiliate with, determine what the term "commonality" entails for that group. Strive to reach an agreement on that goal by reviewing/sorting questionnaire responses followed by the process of discernment to identify steps to take that go beyond where the group is and where the group is heading. Be a provider of light. The area(s) you have chosen is/are where your light will shine. Take steps forward (small/bigger/broad) toward solutions according to group discernment. There are many ways to bring solutions to our common concerns and even to the critical issues of our day.

When setting a pathway to unity within your realm of influence, spend time devising measures and checks to prevent accidental or intentional use of harmful technology or processes that humanity has designed—a method of action that can be directed against humanity (ourselves) and God's creation.

We are now approaching or are at the third "tipping point" of humanity, according to Frank Diana, a contributor to the series "Reimagining the Future" available on YouTube.[3] The historic tipping points are (1) Hunter-gatherer to Agricultural; (2) Agricultural to Industrial (1760); and most recently suggested (3) Industrial to an automated or augmented society, stemming from a Fourth Industrial Revolution that has introduced robotics, Artificial Intelligence (AI), accelerated scientific and technological advances, an increased pace of communications and extensive accessibility to available information/the Internet.[4]

The senior population is a viable source for generating creative and constructive ideas along with other generational groups. Join those who are on a pathway with you toward solutions for a better society. Every segment needs to have its voice.

---

[3] Frank Diana, Reimagining the Future. A Journey Through the Looking Glass—(Views Expressed Are My Own).
Tipping Points in Human History, January 8, 2018.
[4] Although the topic of tipping points is beyond the scope of this book, I include the subject because these pervasive realities may come up in group discussions.

Connecting generations through elder wisdom, story and legacy

Seniors, Irreplaceable Treasures: Here To Be Valued

Story by Jean Marie Albert, an experienced nursing professional

Who are the influencers who have enriched your life and left a lasting impression on you? For me, it started with my grandmother. She was a remarkable woman who taught me invaluable life lessons. She patiently taught me how to cook meals, garden, sew & countless other skills. Because of her, engaging in fun projects & games were a regular occurrence in our daily lives. Being in her presence and witnessing her unwavering faith and exceptional character, influenced me. Nevertheless, it was her particular devotion to caring for the elderly that had a life-altering impact on me. She would take me and my sister to a local long-term care center where she worked as a nurse. We'd visit, help the residents with their daily activities & sometimes, sing songs to entertain them. I remember being stunned by the immense appreciation they showed towards us and how positively they were affected by our attention. I felt a deep sense of connection and belonging there.

At age 18, after high school graduation, I didn't know what to do next. But then I had a vivid dream that gave me direction for my future; I started nurse training toward an LPN license, following in my grandmother's footsteps. As soon as I completed the coursework, I was hired immediately into my first professional job. Amazingly, doors kept opening regularly that allowed me to broaden my skills into other areas of professional development.

Looking back at my career in healthcare, I feel incredibly blessed. Working in rehabilitation, skilled, and long-term care settings, I had the honor of meeting amazing residents who became like stars in my life. They enriched me with their wisdom, resilience, and stories. The laughter and good times we shared still bring me joy. These connections taught me valuable lessons and showed me the benefits & power of intergenerational connection. I am grateful for the privilege of being a part of their lives.

Throughout my life, I've witnessed society's unfortunate tendency to overlook the value of older individuals. However, I firmly believe in the equality of all people and the importance of every individual finding purpose and fulfillment, regardless of their age.

I deeply appreciate the role of a higher power in orchestrating my circumstances and leading me to great opportunities. Secondly, I owe a great deal of my success to the guidance, encouragement, and prayers of the many seniors who have crossed my path. I hold a deep appreciation for the elders I've encountered and those I have yet to meet, as they've played vital roles as coaches, mentors, spiritual guides, and friends. Building proverbial bridges between the older and younger generations brings mutual enrichment. The older generation gains a renewed sense of purpose, energy from interactions, and valuable knowledge about modern technology, while the younger generation benefits from the wisdom, experience, and guidance of their elders.

With this my story concludes, but please do join me on the voyage of embracing intergenerational connections. We will continue to discover priceless treasures.

Connecting generations through elder wisdom, story and legacy

Still life with fruit of the vine. Acrylic, A. Harris.

Mother

Poem by Brenda G. Hall

I look in your eyes, I see you are worn and tired.
I watch you flinch to focus and ask, "Who's there?"
But only to look at me with a stare.

I remember awakening to your breakfast preparation.
I found much joy and gratification.
The familiar breakfast fresh biscuits, eggs, and country bacon.
How could I sleep with such aroma escaping?

Life has taken its toll.
You are now leaning further to the ground.
Don't worry Mom!
I'll take care of you and I won't let you down.

Flowers in Ridged Planter.
Acrylic by A. Harris.

"Blessings Within": Equality Prophesy

by Betty C. Dudney.

Know that you can connect and will eventually connect with a Higher Spiritual Consciousness and be willing to take a fresh look at what you could do with others in responding to the need for people's rights. This focus can bring all the promises of many Blessings Within.

It is obviously going to take the power of many voices and the people's votes in choosing what to support or what not to support, in insisting on fairer ways, insisting on a better life, and a better world. And doing what you decide to do in the best, most positive, non-violent ways not only for your welfare but also for the welfare of all.

What are some of the ways?

Work with other human rights groups either on a local, national, or international level to establish decent living wages as well as equal rights. There are many human rights groups that need people willing to help, support, or network with them and their members.

So, find at least one organization you can trust and believe in. There are organizations that use software to rate non-profits, like "Charity Navigator.com." It is a trustworthy site that gives objective ratings for many groups, some offering opportunities to apply for funding.

Get to know who you are working with. Look for ways to vouch for their work that you believe is making a difference. Not all, but most groups are making a difference! It's important for you to confirm for yourself that the partnership is best for you and your efforts.

It is also good to form small groups of your own, with as few as one or two like-minded friends or co-workers to work in specific areas of similar interest. Stay connected and coordinate efforts toward mutual goals. It only takes one or a few people networking with other groups to keep each other informed as to where the needs are. Your primary efforts should be wherever you feel you have the most to offer and can work with others with God's help. Seek this personal confirmation in working together, be it local, national, or even international in scope.

Our best spiritual gifts, unlike physical gifts, cannot be bought or sold and are only given by God's Holy Spirit to those willing to know and do God's Will. You want to be free from idolatry or a false image of God. Whether you are male or female, weak or strong, big, or small, you are created in God's image for equally good Godly purpose.

You'll first ask forgiveness for any hurt or harm you may have done to yourself, to God, and to others. And then just as importantly, what harm others have done to you.

In giving and receiving this forgiveness, with God's help, you will sense within-- you will know—when you are free from idolatry or any negative influence over you. It may take a long time, or it may seem miraculous to feel the Peace and Joy given by the Holy Spirit when you experience your own "Equality" or Blessings Within.

Connecting generations through elder wisdom, story and legacy

Blessings: Watercolor, by A. Harris.

An Intergalactic Visit

Story by Betty C. Dudney

There are many stories and even studies now of possible life on other planets, in God's universe, that are similar in chemical and geologic conditions to our own planet with its life-giving element, water.

One of my favorite stories was told to me four decades ago by a longtime high school friend, only months before he died in his 50s of cancer. He had not wanted to talk about it before then as he felt he would not be believed.

He confided in me that he came home from college one weekend, several decades earlier to find neighbors gathered outside their homes talking about a spacecraft they had just seen in the sky. This occurrence he doubted very much and went inside his bedroom at the back of the house. He looked out his window onto the backyard, where he saw a small spaceship and a small female figure getting ready to climb up into the craft through a side doorway. She was looking in his direction. Before she entered the ship, he distinctly watched this diminutive figure cross her arms in an X formation in front of her body. She then entered the craft. Within moments, it lifted off the ground.

My friend had never witnessed anything like this before and did not know what to make of it. I made the suggestion, arising out of my Catholic experience, that perhaps her crossed arms were expressing a universal message. That gesture is used when a parishioner desires to receive a blessing from the priest instead of receiving the Holy Eucharist. I believe the space traveler's message to my friend communicated that her visit to Earth was in peace, not to harm. As soon as the visitor entered her craft, it lifted off the ground smoothly and silently, traveling straight up into the sky, and disappearing from view within seconds.

I took my friend's story as a sign that the female traveler came from a planet that honored the female half of its population. But this is my orientation, my perspective, and my purpose: This figure, small in stature, came from a planet in our galaxy that gives females the opportunity to travel the universe and represent an alien population.

And I thought, here we are on Earth, still learning to have respect and provide equal opportunity for the female half of our global community, who represent millions of women around the globe!

It was heartening to me that such representation exists elsewhere in the universe and that universal communication can be possible. Perhaps there will be a day when female humans on Earth will explore the planets and represent our humanity in all its various shapes, sizes, and colors. And where a simple warm smile can mean everything to another being in this world and perhaps beyond.

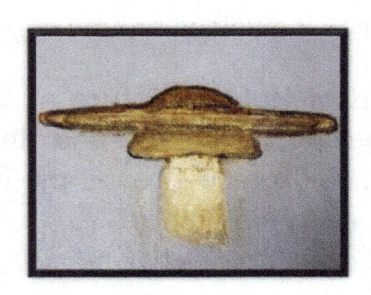

UFO. Acrylic.
A. Harris.

Voices For Our Time:
An Elder's Perspective

By Ann Harris

Several voices of our time seem clearer to me. Developments in technology and advances in medical science have allowed us the know-how to create solutions for today's issues. However future challenges will continue to push the envelope of awareness and knowledge and require a greater depth of understanding.

When asked what event has made the most impact on me within the last 50 years, I'd have to say the past two ongoing years of the COVID pandemic. The actions of many now indicate their belief that COVID is in the past. However, the virus is still present, mutating into new deadly strains. I've written down observations during the pandemic. But what sticks with me are the facts of an unknown outcome, our vulnerability, and a reality of powerlessness. For me, these times shout out a vital call to determine our role in making the world a better place by nurturing our best selves for the society we live in.

For me, the following voices are my current guiding lights.

Contemplation of Holy Scripture at any time, with my Creator God--seeking guidance and thanking God for blessings, mercy, and grace—keeps my life in balance, in focus, and grounded in the Spirit.

The voice of Indigenous peoples/nations.

Indigenous nations have been waiting 400 years for current circumstances to emerge. The vulnerability and culpability of the power society have been exposed through the effects of the COVID pandemic hovering over us for the past two-plus years. Leaders of the indigenous cultures are saying, "The time is now." A time for shaking up the status quo. Generally, most developed nations have not cared well for our earthly homes. Listen to the groans of Mother Earth, the tainted air we breathe, the choked oceans. Many Indigenous groups are in tune with these long-standing issues. Their cultural knowledge can inform us if we listen in gratitude. And respond. Take the steps to repair the damage already heaped upon environmental systems and humanity. Work to bring life on our shared planet back to healthy stasis.

Globally, we are all connected. What happens in one part of the world affects life in another part of the world. Let our sharper awareness, our angst, our technological and scientific know-how, and our intuitive promptings from inner and outer sources guide our responses. I strongly suggest referring to the Pachamama Alliance organization which has for the past 25 years been engaged in linking projects of a global movement to make our planet, our human existence, more environmentally sustainable, spiritually fulfilling, and socially just.[5] Their collaborative work in the Amazon rain

---

[5] Pachamama Alliance website, Pachamama.org. Its mission is to empower indigenous peoples of the Amazon rain forest to preserve their lands and culture, educate and inspire individuals everywhere to bring into being a diverse movement to build a thriving, just and sustainable world. A summary of their Mission is included in Resources.

forest is inspirational and essential for preserving and protecting vital areas from commercial and private developmental gain for a few.

Steven Charleston, Choctaw elder and retired Bishop of the Diocese of Alaska (1991-1996), shares from his book, *Ladder to the Light: An Indigenous Elder's Meditations on Hope and Courage, (Broadleaf Books, January 2021)*. He describes a sacred practice of preparing to enter the community with an informed understanding of seeking common ground with others in our divisive society.

"We share our stories." Ladder to the Light, The Rung of Transformation (pp 123-124).

"When we share our questions together, we become our own answer. We discover that there is no one right way to do everything. We understand that no single plan will encompass the way forward. If we seek to bring light into darkness, then we must rely on the wisdom of us all. We listen to one another. We are patient with one another. We spend time with one another. Eventually, we trust one another because we see ourselves in one another. In other words, we go into the kiva together. We return to our place of beginning. We find our common ground. We share our stories."

"We emerged from Mother Earth." "Ladder to the Light, Introduction: The Vision of the Kiva (p. 7ff).

"Kiva: The kiva is a square or circular underground chamber covered by a roof of wooden beams with an opening in the center. You enter a kiva the same way you enter a submarine by descending the ladder. Once inside the packed earth chamber of the kiva, you are in darkness. Without a fire in the kiva, the only light comes from above you. To reach it, you have to ascend the ladder. The kiva is a sacred place."

"The kiva symbolizes spiritual resilience. It reminds us that we began in darkness, not the stark, ominous darkness we imagine we face today, but the nurturing darkness of the womb, a place of formation and growth. Over time, through the grace of the Spirit, we learned more, understood more, until we matured and were ready to take our place in the bright world of reality. We emerged from Mother Earth.":

"The vision of the kiva is not just for Native Americans, but for all who will receive it. It is a symbol of our shared future."

Academic voices of science and medicine.

A retired lab technologist friend shares, "Viruses will cause significant challenges in global health and welfare. A rampant, unchecked virus can eliminate entire populations."

Scientific/medical responses to such a pandemic reveal deep ethical issues at the core of our society. These issues (elitism, inequality/inequity, racial oppression), if not resolved, remain ever-present, either in the foreground of awareness (like now) or as seen in media coverage of public demonstrations and social justice pronouncements on streets across our nation (like now). There are times when these issues linger just as potently in the background of current events, waiting for an opportunity to come into the light once again. Let's grab this opportunity of "now" and seek improvement of the human condition. Face the issues now while they are in the light, or through passive inaction, they will return to the background of events until their next emergence.

A cautionary voice for the health of our republic.

The pandemic brought to light our human vulnerability. Daily lives as we know them, have been modified. It seems that the basic tenets of equality and opportunity, on which our nation was formed, are being tested.

The voice of prophetic spirituality.

"The prophet is a person who says "no" to everything that is not of God:"

No to abuse of women.
    the rejection of the stranger.
    crimes against immigrants.
    the pollution of the skies.
    the poisoning of the oceans.
    the destruction of humankind.
    for the sake of more wealth,
    more power, more control for a few.
"The prophet is one who speaks the truth to a culture of lies,

Yes to equal rights for all.
    embracing the different.
    who God made you.
    embracing life.
    the pursuit of wholeness.
    acceptance of others."[6]
    (Joan Chittister, "The Time is Now," p.15-16)

---

[6] *The Time is Now: a call to uncommon courage* by Joan Chittister, OSB. Convergent Books. Crown Publishing Group, a division of Penguin Random House, LLC, New York, 2019.

How do we exist peacefully together? Globalism is now a daily reminder of co-existence and a shared planet. Technology has brought all corners of the world into our living rooms. We cannot be ignorant of global needs and the necessity of living peacefully with others.

The voice of a poet.

Excerpts: Amanda Gorman's inaugural poem, Jan. 20, 2021. (The first Youth Poet Laureate):[7]

The Hill We Climb

Somehow, we've weathered and witnessed a nation that isn't broken but simply unfinished.

We are striving to forge a union with purpose, to compose a country committed to all cultures, colors, characters and conditions of man.

And so, we lift our gazes not to what stands between us, but what stands before us.
The hill we climb if only we dare it,
because being American is more than a pride we inherit—
it's the past we step into
and how we repair it.

When day comes, we step out of the shade, aflame and unafraid.
The new dawn blooms as we free it.

---

[7] Amanda Gorman, First Youth Poet Laureate read her poem "The Hill We Climb" at Joe Biden's presidential inauguration, Jan. 20, 2021. See Resources for full text.

For there is always light.
If only we are brave enough to see it.
If only we're brave enough to be it.

The hopeful, life-giving voice of God's Mercy
as expressed by Catherine McAuley, Foundress of the Sisters of Mercy in this verse:

Sweet Mercy…not easily provoked, she soon forgives, feels love for all, and by a look relieves.
Soft peace she brings wherever she arrives, removes the anguish and reforms our lives, making the rough paths of peevish nature even, and opens in each heart a little heaven." [8]

For me, these are the voices of our time. I pray that I can "be brave enough to be it" and seek holy guidance. Do you hear them, or different voices? Voices that are distinct from the cacophony of hatred, separation, and untruths? What do they lead you to do and be?

---

[8] Sweet Mercy," poem by Catherine McAuley, RSM, Foundress of the Sisters of Mercy in Dublin, Ireland, 1831

Amaryllis. Acrylic, A. Harris.

The Bay: A Sacred Place

Story by Ann Harris

Alice found herself at the edge of a clearing. Behind her was the short trail back to the island's rocky shoreline. In front of her was an open field. At the far end were several women chanting around a smoking campfire.

Sensing the presence of a stranger, the women stopped their song. A bundle held high over the rising smoke was lowered and carried quickly into the thicket behind them. All disappeared from view.

As Alice watched them move out of sight, an object fell to the ground unnoticed beside the fire. The clearing was now empty and silent. She approached the firepit, retraced her steps back to the dinghy, and returned to *Bonne Isle*.

***

Alice's mother watched her daughter sitting by the cabin window, staring out over the sparkling waters of the Bay. She was used to her teenager's mood swings back in the city, but this was their summer haven, a blissful time of relaxation on their island *Bonne Isle* at Georgian Bay, two hours north of the city. What was on Alice's troubled mind as she sat so still in thought?

Her hand felt the edges of the object in her jeans pocket. Alice finally spoke,

"I'm going back to the island where I was a couple of days ago, Mom. There's something I need to know."

"Be careful navigating the Bay, dear. The water level is 10 inches down this summer."

"I have the water depth maps with me, Mom. Don't worry. I've taken my dinghy around the islands and know where the shoals are. I'll be back before too long."

Sitting in the stern of her boat at the end of the floating dock, Alice pulled the power cord to the outboard motor. The engine purred. She reached into her jeans pocket and pulled out the necklace. A short, shiny silver chain held a silver medallion encrusted with agates and precious stones. An encryption of some sort was etched on the reverse side. It was so beautiful she couldn't leave it on the ground by the fire.

Yesterday she asked several local islanders what this object was. Eddie at the marina knew a lot about Bay history and the First Nation people who settled and still lived in the area. "Miss Alice, this looks like ceremonial jewelry of the tribe who lives around here. Some of their ways are mysterious…in a spirit kind of way."

Sam, an old islander for more than 50 years, warned, "I wouldn't hold on to it, Miss Alice. No tellin' what powers it may have."

Alice put the necklace back in her jeans pocket and pushed away from the dock. She headed straight across the Bay to the island she discovered two days ago. She walked the short woodland path to the open clearing and paused, watching. As she drew nearer to the cool fire pit, an old woman appeared suddenly out from the thick brush.

Startled by her sudden appearance, Alice wondered, *has this woman been waiting here-- for days perhaps? Was she waiting for me?*

The woman's forehead was deeply wrinkled across her brow, but the dark skin around her mouth and cheeks was smooth and youthful. Her gray hair was thickly braided and hung down her back to her waist. As she approached, Alice smelled her delicately beaded leather vest and heard the rustle of her long skirt, handwoven with colorful threads. Her face---her face was glowing, open, and friendly. Deep black eyes shone brightly, strongly pulling Alice's attention toward her.

The woman smiled and reached out inviting Alice's hands to join hers, as she quietly explained,

"Two days ago, a baby was being received into the tribal community by women elders through our ancient Welcoming Ways: smoke to cleanse the newborn spirit, songs of praise to the Creator, and a sign of membership into the life of the tribe—a bead and agate silver medallion made by the women."

"There's no need to fear what you have seen or what you have done, young miss. It is a beautiful ceremony that was interrupted by you, a stranger, unfamiliar with our ways."

Alice placed the necklace in the woman's hands and she accepted it with unspoken gratitude. In a few moments, the two women left each other's company strangers no longer.

Alice laughed with a new lightness of spirit as she drove her dinghy across the Bay waters towards *Bonne Isle*. She ran up the dirt footpath to the cabin and shared her encounter with her mother. After Alice finished telling what had happened, her mother responded, "It sounds like two sacred places were restored today: a tribal ceremonial site and your beautiful heart, my dear daughter."

*Georgian Bay windswept pine.
Acrylic by A. Harris.*

Loss of Innocence

Story by Bobbi Albert

The two women participants looked around the room and wondered what they were doing there on this sunny Saturday at a workshop on biological and chemical terrorism. Did the ten other people in attendance know why they were there? Or were they just as clueless? In truth, the only person who really understood the gravity of the subject was the presenter, Dr. Raymond Miller. Dr. Miller, a member of the National Guard, was a known expert on acts of terrorism worldwide, and specifically on intelligence threats against the United States. According to him, acts of biological and chemical terrorism against the United States were not a matter of if, but when.

Two young women entered the State Public Health Laboratory building where their offices were located. The building was a large, red brick structure that had originally been a tuberculosis hospital back in the day when TB patients went to sanitoriums to recuperate. Now it housed the laboratories that performed biologic and chemical testing for the State of Tennessee and was a liaison with the Centers for Disease Control and Prevention. As they entered the lobby their attention was drawn to the television set above the entrance desk. It showed an airplane careening into a tall building. What was going on? They stood frozen watching an attack on a building in New York City. They both flashed back to Dr. Miller's lecture a month ago.

9/11/2001. A day that is imprinted into the psyche of most Americans as the day that terrorism became a reality, the day "if" became "now." And while the destruction of the World Trade Center was a horrendous act of aggression, it was also a stark reminder that terrorism encompassed not only specific focal acts but also the threat of biological and chemical terrorism. The United States, and indeed, the world, had entered a new era...an era where countries and civilizations could be destroyed by micro-organisms or chemicals.

The workshop that was so underattended had happened a month ago. Since then, at Dr. Miller's insistence, another workshop had been planned, this one in Tennessee, and up until this day on 9/11 had only five participants registered. Suddenly registration exploded. Within days the workshop reached capacity. And more were planned—multiple workshops in every state and for many years. It was imperative that laboratory technologists be trained to identify the microorganisms used for bioterrorism and the chemicals used in chemical terrorism.

Our world has lived with the uneasy knowledge of the horrors that can be unleashed with the use of biological and chemical agents for some time now. Has this knowledge and awareness dwindled to complacency? If so, these are shades of 9/11. Let's not be lulled into non-attention when real threats are aired on the evening news. This time by a world leader who is threatening to use these agents against a country he wants to subdue and conquer. What will be the outcome if this action is undertaken by this madman? Let's not be caught off-guard by complacency, by a passive response.

Surely, the responsible nations of the world have a plan to block such madness. I'd occupy the first row at a workshop that provides information on established checks on such irresponsible, deadly leadership. Sign me up Dr. Miller!

Lion and lamb. Acrylic by A. Harris.

Estuary—a place of culmination, imagination, and creative gift: An Interpretation

By Ann Harris

**Old Age: the estuary that enlarges and spreads Itself grandly as it pours into the Great Sea.
Walt Whitman**

Walt Whitman's image of Old Age is a poignant one. If life is imagined as a river, flowing, gathering, releasing, building up, creating, and reducing, over a span of decades, the culmination of experience that occurs as one approaches the estuary, is the inevitable pouring of the river into a larger expanse—the sea. The estuary, where the contained freshwater riverbanks meet the powerful, tidal, salty Great Sea, becomes the mixing, remixing, tumbling, transforming place of the individual's life. The elderly can be exposed to an enlargement of the panorama—a fresh open canvas on which to create, share, build, restore, recreate, and ultimately release. A fertile growing place where life experiences meld or become more informed in understanding and enlightenment-- if one is open to this opportunity.

John Denver in his album, The Muppets, sings a sweet lyrical song written by Paul H. Williams, "When the River Meets the Sea" that gives context to a person's heightened understanding when entering the place where the river meets the sea. One stanza says,

> *Though our minds be filled with questions*
> *in our hearts we'll understand*
> *when the river meets the sea.*

In the Resources section are the full lyrics of "When the River Meets the Sea." Use the following online address to listen to this song sung by John Denver and The Muppets, in the Christmas album "A Christmas Together" aired in December, 1979. This album won The Grammy Award for Best Album for Children in 1979.

https://www.youtube.com/watch?v=H2Qm2uPJx-8

A March 1, 2024 commentary by Chelsea Rush, a frequent contributor to OldTimeMusic, says in her article on "The Meaning Behind the Song: When the River Meets the Sea by Paul Williams:"

"This song's lyrics speak to the eternal cycles of life and the interconnectedness of all things. It beautifully captures the profoundness and mystery of existence, inviting listeners to contemplate the deeper meaning behind the flow of time and the inevitability of change."

"Furthermore, "When the River Meets the Sea" emphasizes the importance of patience and acceptance. It acknowledges that the answers to life's most profound questions may not always be readily available, but they will reveal themselves in due time. In that final hour, truth and justice will prevail." The song's words are timeless, very relevant for today and full of hope for the generations of our time and beyond.

It is God's gift to revel in this expansiveness. In a retirement environment, there is most likely additional personal time to examine new directions and ideas, revisit old ones, and be open to new expressions and passions that perhaps have been part of a life for a long time yet have remained unexplored, unexamined, unexpressed. It is a time of opening, discovery, invitation, a freeing. These are the positive gifts at this time of life which can be shared richly with family, and others. For all age groups, how beautiful it can be to seek out these gifts of elder years.

The effect of the estuary is magical and surprising, but perhaps also fearful for the moment because of the newness of revelation. An individual can use and share these skills and abilities or not. As one becomes more and more part of the Great Sea, gradually losing one's individual identity while gaining a broader understanding of the world and one's community, God's purpose is served in humility and gratitude. The gifts the Creator has bestowed on each person during one's lifetime are forged, modified, enhanced, diminished, and built up as life experiences are lived and developed-- or not.

The estuary is a place where enlarged gifts of self and others are unfolding and coalescing, as is the purpose of the God-filled life until one's essence becomes one with the Great Sea and Legacy is preserved for future generations.

Ode to the Estuary

Poem by Ann Harris

Come, dear friend, let's go, side-by-side
to enter together the sea-driven tides
where the estuary presses around us now.
I feel welcome as Spirit shows us how
to treat one another, and strangers, too,
with kindness, in everything we do.
We're challenged with love and grace
in this-- God's vast and merciful place.

Oh! How beautiful spending elder time here
in the presence of Spirit, where there's no fear?
Strengths we have nurtured over decades of days,
relieve all pain, entering gently into play.
We're tossed and tumbled by the rumbling surf,
exhilarated; disturbing beliefs from our birth.
Rethinking, revising, what we've learned to date.
These changes are welcome, and not too late.

We believe Spirit has brought us life anew
fostering a better world; we try, and hope it's true.
Revelations around us are accepted by a few,
like candy tossed by passersby to a crowd within view.
Some pick it up and cherish the message at its core.
Others leave it--unclaimed--strewn on life's busy floor.

Such is the randomness which opportunity proffers.
Receiver must be ready to accept the gift that's offered,
allowing the fruit to flourish,
and too, the seed of meaning.
Let the blossoms bloom, and the seed be redeeming.

Connecting generations through elder wisdom, story and legacy

The estuary--where our legacies coalesce--
moves us closer so that God may bless
us on our journey toward the horizon ahead.
Into its radiant Spirit, we are being led.

*Starfish near the estuary
where the river meets the sea.
Acrylic, A. Harris.*

A New Day Arises from COVID

By Ann Harris

March 2020

COVID-19 arrives, stirs up, and flips our daily living. Old patterns no longer apply. Citizens and friends are dying of the deadly virus. Seniors are labeled at particular risk. Federal health measures earmark the elderly segment of society as needing to be protected through isolation, and behavioral controls that bring confusion into the daily lives of the older adult who is living in a senior residence. Entrance doors are locked, closing off family contacts. Society at large regroups under federal health guidelines. Vaccines are manufactured to combat the pandemic. New deadly strains arise requiring updated medical prescriptions. Meanwhile, the future welfare of our planet is uncertain. Signs all around us are pointing to ill health.

March 2023

A new day is here calling for our attention arising from the insecurities of the pandemic and the changed ways of daily living it forged.

We are becoming more aware that foundational changes in how we conduct our lives are on the horizon. As caretakers of the planet, our common home, we are called to attend to our world in ways we've never done before. How do we build a better more equitable, just, safer, and healthier tomorrow?

Hopefully, together, bravely—with our Guide by our side.

New paradigms based on collaboration and healing are

entering our reality. Movements to rebuild a healthier environment are the strength of the world to come. The elderly population is as strong as other segments of society as participants in the new contexts.

A movement that has been mentioned previously, the Pachamama Alliance, which links indigenous wisdom with modern knowledge and technology, offers an enlightening two-hour free course, "Awakening the Dreamer: Changing the Dream," that takes an honest look at the challenging state of the world.

Holy Scripture tells us that we have within us from our Creator everything necessary to do great things. We are being called to prayerfully dig deeply within, to humbly access it, ... to courageously draw upon it ... and to BE IT

It's time to prepare ourselves for these life-changing shifts and join the healing, unifying movements that have formed and are forming around us—being open to the universal Spirit available to all and necessary for a sustainable life.

CONCLUSION

The experience of the Estuary is real, challenging, somewhat scary, yet ultimately exciting and satisfying. It means being aware as fully as possible of where you are, where you are going, for today—just for today. Your destination may be unknown; but if you keep your basic foundations, the change agents that are forming around you will enhance the beautiful tapestry of your life being woven by you day to day, and not overwhelm you.

All we really know is the Now. The Holy Spirit is with us every hour, guiding our searching, and our growing. Isn't that reality the best adventure we can experience no matter what our conditions may be?

So, seniors, and every human being on earth, keep traveling on in courage and hope. Keep writing about your lives, seeing what gifts, discoveries, and understandings are revealed to you along the way until the sweet moment when your spirit joins the glorious Great Sea and your legacies live on.

A Trio of Pears. Acrylic, A. Harris.

Connecting generations through elder wisdom, story and legacy

REFLECTION ON SENIOR STATEMENTS AND IMAGES
with Commentary by the Late Fred Rogers
The Late Fred Rogers on the Importance of Taking Time

The words of TV personality Fred Rogers gave children on the set of Mr. Rogers' Neighborhood the gift of reflection, remembrance, and silence. He used the noisy medium, television, to teach about silence and slowing down. He considered silence his most important legacy. He invited his television neighbor to sit and take a moment to think about the beauty of things—a piece of music, a poem, an animal, a plant, a shared painting or drawing—and take a moment to thank the God who inspires and informs us about all that is nourishing and good.[9]

"It seems to me that our world needs more time to wonder and to reflect about what is inside, and if we take time, we can often go much deeper as far as our spiritual life is concerned than we can if there's a constant distraction. And often television gives such constant distraction—noise and fast-paced things—which doesn't allow us to take time to explore the deeper levels of who we are—and who we can become."

---

[9] The Simple Faith of Mister Rogers: spiritual insights from the world's most beloved neighbor, Amy Hollingsworth. The importance of taking time, p. 4-5, 2005: Integrity Publishers: Brentwood, TN.

Opportunity for Discussion

Looking at the elderly from a positive, participatory perspective, the statements below are presented as an opportunity for discussion within the family circle, with friends and groups.

1. What are your thoughts about these statements or images?
2. Which statements ring "true" or "false" in your experience wherever you are on the life spectrum?
3. How does Fred Rogers' commentary resonate with you?
4. How does our culture respond to his coaching?
5. Does your living reflect his urging for silence and time for reflection?
6. Are these factors important to you in your life?

I invite you to revisit these questions and the following statements/images when you have considered the content of this writing. Have your conceptions changed to any degree? If so, how?

***

Lifelong living gives valuable perspective to setting personal priorities according to new or long-standing interests.

Elder years embrace lifelong ways of living embodying life lessons that youth and middle years can learn from, to their benefit, appreciate, enjoy, and sincerely honor.

Elders have reached a place where there is more freedom to be oneself and to choose what will fill their days without undo concern about what others think.

For many elders, each day presents a challenge to respond to invitations for new adventures ... to decide where to put their energies.

An elder is likely to handmake a quilt or bed blanket for family members as a gift of love and labor to be enjoyed and cherished for generations.

An elder writes a thoughtful note of thanks or friendship with an unsteady hand.

Senior life is often a rich time for self-discovery and a time of courage to receive and share what is waiting to be revealed.

The elder years are open to new discoveries and understandings amidst a diminishing scope of activities.

Elders display daily courage amidst dimming eyesight, slippage of memory, and ambulatory aids.

An elder's daily living is no longer continuous, automatic actions but those of focused energy and commitment.

An outer/external elder figure is made up of many smaller forms fitting perfectly over each other, each with time markers of learning, being, and creativity that over time create a unique set of well-fitting figures.

An elder expertly knits a baby cap and booties for a precious perfect newborn baby lovingly given from a precious imperfect body perhaps with arthritic hands.

An elder gains the satisfaction of living out fully the final pages of one's own storybook.

The elder time of life can provide a less stressful framework for living as compared to the responsibilities of homemaking and the workplace and their former demands.

The elder gives the gift of creating cherished legacies and memories for the next generation and beyond.

Connecting generations through elder wisdom, story and legacy

Dear Reader,

I invite you to jot down on the lined paper below notes about your reading experience: sections that catch your interest, phrases you would like to share with others, and maybe begin your own commentary on issues raised in these pages. Perhaps some senior statements on previous pages encourage you to delve a little deeper, as Fred Rogers suggests. Ann Harris

Notes

_____
_____
_____
_____
_____
_____
_____
_____
_____

Connecting generations through elder wisdom, story and legacy

Grateful for the gifts of contributors to Rewiring Not Retiring: Connecting generations through elder wisdom, story and legacy.

Contributing Authors

Shoshana Abraham, PhD. Shoshana is a Biblical (Old and New Testaments) interpreter, speaker and teacher specializing in Hebraisms and Prophetical Writings bridging the gap between Jews and Christians, inspiring and preparing this "journey" into the New Promised Land. She lives in Nashville at the Villa.

Bobbi Albert Bobbi lives at the Villa and has participated in the VMM writing group from its beginning. She is a natural teller of stories and has contributed several writings about her life and beliefs arising from her life-long experiences and a long-term career as a professional medical laboratory technologist.

Jean Marie Albert With over 20 years of experience in the healthcare field, Jean Marie is a former writer of case studies that highlighted healing journeys. She is currently a content creator on social media platforms. She finds joy in writing to inspire others.

Lisa Atkinson Lisa is a born storyteller. Many of her writings have been in the legal field, but she has begun to tap into entertaining stories from her childhood and adult life that give family and friends much to smile about.

Wanda Bumpus Wanda's poem was written on her eightieth birthday, celebrated in royal style with over 60 relatives and friends in attendance. Wanda is a writer and creative individual who is always involved in an artistic project. Wanda served as past president of the Villa Maria Resident Council.

Laima Dickens Laima has recently earned her Spiritual Practitioner License through extensive study at the Center for Spiritual Living in East Nashville. Her lifelong courageous journey is an inspiration to all who have experienced and survived extreme challenges in life.

Betty C. Dudney Betty, a resident of the Villa, has shared her Prophesy of Equality in her published, "Blessings Within Equality Prophecy (2021). This profound message was placed on her heart by a powerful encounter with God earlier in her spiritual journey.

Sue Duplessis Sue has lived in Nashville for decades. She grew up in Louisiana within the Cajun community. Her profession was in healthcare and she finds Villa Maria Manor a satisfying place where she can apply her life experiences in meaningful ways in her elder years.

Brenda G. Hall Brenda Hall is a native Nashvillian and is the author of a self-published book, "A Collection of Poems by Brenda G. Hall." Her poem "Mother" is included in the collection.

Connecting generations through elder wisdom, story and legacy

Ann Harris Ann Harris has called Nashville "home" since 1980. Leaving the academic setting in 2000, Ann worked many years in nonprofit management having earned her Master's in Science/Counseling and nonprofit management certificate from Tennessee State University. Ann developed a love for painting and writing in her late 60s and encourages creative self-expression at any age. She has served as an Elder at Westminster Presbyterian Church in Nashville, remains an active member there, and cherishes her long connection with the Sisters of Mercy as a Mercy Associate.

Juliette McMahon Juliette is a resident of the Villa. She has served as an officer for Hospitality on the Villa Maria Manor Resident Council. She is known for her varied interests and active participation in many activities of the residence.

Brenda Nichols Brenda has lived in Nashville since 2 010 and contributes actively to making crafts and writing stories with the Villa Writing Group. Visit the Villa's sales tables to see Brenda's creations; also enjoy her delightful shared stories!

Annie Pardo Annie grew up in France where many of her engaging stories take place. She participates in the Villa writers' group and spends her time with family members in the Nashville area.

RESOURCES

Page 4. Preface

Advisement in planning for the care of aging loved ones:

Connect with resources through a financial advisor to assist in planning and caring for aging parents and loved ones. Discuss estate planning that includes care for older persons such as advice on tax returns, avoidance of financial fraud, social and banking involvement, Power of Attorney, costs of residential living, insurance and health care policies, necessary legal documentation--advance directives and health care proxy.

Having these discussions and putting a plan in place, covering as many of these issues as possible, will ease the management of a loved one's elder years.

Page 97. Pachamama Alliance. Its global focus and programs.

The Pachamama Alliance's Mission, Vision and Purpose

JANUARY 04, 2013 | BY LILIANA M. PELIKS

Mission

Our mission is to empower the indigenous people of the Amazon rainforest to preserve their lands and culture *and, using insights gained from that work,* to educate and inspire individuals everywhere to bring forth a thriving, just, and sustainable world.

Connecting generations through elder wisdom, story and legacy

Vision

The vision that informs The Pachamama Alliance's work is of a world that works for everyone: an environmentally sustainable, spiritually fulfilling, socially just human presence on this planet -- a New Dream for humanity.

Purpose

The Pachamama Alliance, empowered by our partnership with indigenous people, is dedicated to bringing forth an environmentally sustainable, spiritually fulfilling, socially just human presence on this planet.

Our unique contribution is to generate and engage people everywhere in transformational conversations and experiences consistent with this purpose. We weave together indigenous and modern worldviews such that human beings are in touch with their dignity and are ennobled by the magnificence, mystery, and opportunity of what is possible for humanity at this time.

We are here to inspire and galvanize the human family to generate a critical mass of conscious commitment to a thriving, just, and sustainable way of life on Earth. This is a commitment to transforming human systems and structures that separate us, and to transforming our relationships with ourselves, with one another, and with the natural world.

Page 101, Voices for our time; an elder's perspective. ***Following is the full text of Amanda Gorman's poem read at President Biden's inauguration on January 20, 2021.***

The Hill We Climb

A poem by Amanda Gorman

When day comes we ask ourselves,
'where can we find light in this never-ending shade,'
the loss we carry,
a sea we must wade?
We've braved the belly of the beast.
We've learned that quiet isn't always peace,
and the norms and notions
of what just is
isn't always just ice.
And yet the dawn is ours
before we knew it,
somehow we do it.
Somehow we've weathered and witnessed
a nation that isn't broken
but simply unfinished.
We, the successors of a country and a time
where a skinny Black girl
descended from slaves and raised by a single mother
can dream of becoming president
only to find herself reciting for one.
And yes, we are far from polished,
far from pristine,
but that doesn't mean we are
striving to form a union that is perfect.
We are striving to forge a union with purpose,
to compose a country committed to all cultures, colors,
characters, and
conditions of man.
And so we lift our gazes not to what stands between us
but what stands before us.

Connecting generations through elder wisdom, story and legacy

We close the divide because we know, to put our future first,
we must first put our differences aside.
We lay down our arms
so we can reach out our arms
to one another.
We seek harm to none and harmony for all.
Let the globe, if nothing else, say this is true:
That even as we grieved, we grew;
that even as we hurt, we hoped;
that even as we tried, we tried;
that we'll forever be tied together, victorious,
not because we will never again know defeat
but because we will never again sow division.
Scripture tells us to envision
that everyone shall sit under their own vine and fig tree
and no one shall make them afraid.
If we're to live up to our own time
then victory won't lie in the blade
but in all the bridges we've made.
That is the promise to glade,
the hill we climb
if only we dare it,
because being American is more than a pride we inherit —
it's the past we step into
and how we repair it.
We've seen a force that would shatter our nation
rather than share it
would destroy our country if it meant delaying democracy.
And this effort very nearly succeeded.
But while democracy can be periodically delayed,
it can never be permanently defeated.
In this truth,
in this faith we trust,

for while we have our eyes on the future,
history has its eyes on us.
This is the era of just redemption
we feared at its inception.
We did not feel prepared to be the heirs
of such a terrifying hour
but within it, we found the power
to author a new chapter,
to offer hope and laughter to ourselves.
So once we asked,
'how could we possibly prevail over catastrophe,'
now we assert,
'how could catastrophe possibly prevail over us?'
We will not march back to what was
but move to what shall be:
a country that is bruised but whole,
benevolent but bold,
fierce, and free.
We will not be turned around
or interrupted by intimidation
because we know our inaction and inertia
will be the inheritance of the next generation.
Our blunders become their burdens.
But one thing is certain:
If we merge mercy with might,
and might with right,
then love becomes our legacy
and change our children's birthright.
So let us leave behind a country
better than the one we were left with.
Every breath from my bronze-pounded chest,
we will raise this wounded world into a wondrous one.
We will rise from the gold-limned hills of the west,

we will rise from the windswept northeast
where our forefathers first realized revolution,
we will rise from the lake-rimmed cities of the midwestern
states,
we will rise from the sunbaked south.
We will rebuild, reconcile, and recover
in every known nook of our nation and
every corner called our country,
our people diverse and beautiful will emerge,
battered and beautiful.
When the day comes we step out of the shade,
aflame and unafraid.
The new dawn blooms as we free it.
For there is always light,
if only we're brave enough to see it,
if only we're brave enough to be it.

Page 112. John Denver, popular singer/songwriter in the 1970s and 80s, sings When the River Meets the Sea (written by Paul H. Williams) in The Muppets album "A Christmas Together," released December 1979. Full lyrics follow.

When the River Meets the Sea

When the mountain touches the valley
all the clouds are taught to fly,
as our souls will leave this land most peacefully

Though our minds be filled with questions,
in our hearts we'll understand
when the river meets the sea.

Like a flower that has blossomed
in dry and barren sand,
we are born and born again most gracefully.

Plus, the winds of time will take us
with a sure and steady hand
when the river meets the sea.

Patience, my brother and patience, my son.
In that sweet and final hour
truth and justice will be done.

Like a baby when it is sleeping
in its loving mother's arms
what a newborn baby dreams, is a mystery.

But his life will find a purpose
and in time, he'll understand
when the river meets the sea.
When the river meets the almighty sea.